HAIRSPRAY™

What gives a girl
power and punch?

Is it charm, is it poise?
No, it's...

HAIRSPRAY ™

Foreword by John Waters

Director's Notes by Adam Shankman

Introduction by Craig Zadan & Neil Meron

Mama Edna's Turn by John Travolta

Photographs by David James

Text by Diana Landau

Insight Editions
17 Paul Drive
San Rafael, CA 94903
800.688.2218
415.526.1370
Fax: 415.526.1394
www.insighteditions.com

NEW LINE CINEMA
A Time Warner Company

Library of Congress Cataloging-in-Publication
Data available.

ISBN-10 1-933784-38-5
ISBN-13 9781933784-38-0

GLOBAL
RELEAF   ⊕ REPLANTED PAPER

Palace Press International, in association with Global
ReLeaf™, will plant two trees for each tree used in
the manufacturing of this book. Global ReLeaf™ is an
international campaign by American Forests, the nation's
oldest nonprofit conservation organization and a world
leader in planting trees for environmental restoration.

Printed in China by Palace Press International
www.palacepress.com

10 9 8 7 6 5 4 3 2 1

c o n t e n t s

part one

Making Hairspray

"For me, the trick to making
this movie work was that
Tracy never stops hearing
music in her head."

— *Director Adam Shankman*

Hairspray Goes Hollywood

by John Waters

Here we go again. *Hairspray 3? Hairspray II? Hairspray the Movie Musical?* How about just good old-fashioned *Hairspray?* Boy, am I flattered that a story I thought up sitting on the bed in my old apartment in an upper-lower-class neighborhood in Baltimore has been reinvented *again*, and in such a spectacular way. First came my movie, much closer to a documentary than many realized—except that no fat girl was *ever* a regular on *The Buddy Deane Show*, the local TV dance party that inspired my screenplay. Then my movie was turned into a Broadway musical, directed by Jack O'Brian with music by Marc Shaiman and Scott Wittman. And now Hollywood (well, New Line Cinema *is* Hollywood today, but they had about six employees when I first started doing business with them in 1972) has reinvented the musical as a big-budget, all-star summer blockbuster. (*Not* in the old, racially tense sense of this word.)

I remember being driven up to the new set of Baltimore in Toronto and feeling slightly stupefied. Yes, I knew Maryland had lost the production due to a lack of soundstages big enough in which to film the elaborate musical numbers, but still—here was my hometown reproduced in another country. Oh well, at least it wasn't Bucharest, Romania, a city that aggressively chases runaway American productions and is even cheaper to film in than Toronto. Even Maryland Film Commissioner Jack Gerbes, trying to be a gracious loser, joked, "After all, the producers Craig Zadan and Neil Meron did produce *Chicago* in Toronto and that won the Oscar."

I was proud that director Adam Shankman asked me to do a cameo as "The Flasher." At least I could stay true to my image. Adam had come to Baltimore for research, and I had given him the *Hairspray* tour of East Baltimore—the aorta of beehive history. After our field trip, I knew he understood my unironic appreciation of the neighborhood and wanted to keep my off-kilter love of the

Above: John Waters with director Adam Shankman and Nikki Blonsky on the Baltimore set.
Opposite: Waters in character as "The Flasher" encounters the beauty shop ladies.

extreme in the new film, no matter how high the budget. When I read the funny screenplay by Leslie Dixon, I closed my eyes, thought about artistic magic (and a passive income), and prayed that creative lightning could strike three times in a row.

Some things on location felt the same. Sitting in John Travolta's trailer as he got into costume and makeup as Edna did give me flashbacks to both Divine and Harvey Feinstein going through the laborious process. Luckily for Mr. Travolta, the fat-suit prosthetic, which started just under his chin and continued downward, cut down on his body-shaving torture. Tony Gardner, the amazing special effects wizard who worked with me on making Selma Blair's giant bosom for *A Dirty Shame*, is an old pro at making talent feel comfortable even while distorting their real figures. Together he and Travolta came up with a new body for Edna, one that is just as startlingly frumpy and lovable as the past models; but so seamless that Travolta could embrace his new girth and use it to turn Edna into a character all his own.

Seeing the new *Hairspray* must be strangest for the real "Buddy Deaners"— the regulars from the Baltimore TV show, who not only helped Ed Love (who choreographed my film) learn the real-life dances for that film but are helping promote the new one by giving interviews for the documentary on the whole *Hairspray* phenomenon, to be included on the eventual DVD. Arlene Kozak was the one-time supervisor of the show's teen stars, some of whom say that she still rules them with a loving iron fist. When my assistant called to ask if she wanted to participate, the nearly 70-year-old Arlene admitted she was going through some serious health issues, then warily asked, "Who's gonna play me in the movie this time?" When my assistant replied, "Michelle Pfeiffer," Arlene laughed out loud: "You've made my day." And you know what? I think the new *Hairspray* will make yours, too.

"I was proud that director Adam Shankman asked me to do a cameo as 'The Flasher.' At least I could stay true to my image."

— John Waters

Reinventing the Movie Musical

By Craig Zadan and Neil Meron

People have said from the start that we're absolutely out of our minds for taking on the movie musical genre and that movie musicals died out two or three decades ago because audiences lost interest in them. It's true that at a certain point Hollywood became very averse to these movies and many of them failed to attract audiences. But we have a different idea about why that happened—and why the genre is having such a renaissance now, with wonderful films like *Moulin Rouge*, *Chicago*, *Dreamgirls*, and, of course, *Hairspray*.

What really happened is that filmmakers weren't adept at making movie musicals that worked. Even when the material was good, musicals often failed to make the leap from stage to screen, because people tried to simply "recreate" rather than "reinvent" the Broadway experience—thinking that you could just take a musical from the stage, point a camera at it, and film it. But that never really works. Many have fallen into this trap, and it's understandable. You might try to religiously recreate every moment from a stage show, which may please the show's devoted fans but completely shuts out moviegoing audiences who have never seen it.

Our goal is always to honor the original material, do it justice—yet reinvent it and introduce it to a whole new group of people who, in this case, have no prior experience of seeing the *Hairspray* story. We are huge fans of the classic John Waters movie and the Broadway show, both of which succeed brilliantly on their own terms. But to make this work as a movie musical, we had to look at it with fresh eyes.

Our long experience in filming musicals includes three highly rated productions for TV: *Gypsy*, with Bette Midler; *Cinderella*, with Whitney Houston and Brandy; and *Annie*, with Kathy Bates. Theatrically, our production of *Chicago* was the first movie musical in 34 years to win the Best Picture Oscar and was the highest-grossing movie in the history of Miramax Films. These experiences

Producer Craig Zadan, Zac Efron (Link Larkin), producer Neil Meron, and James Marsden (Corny Collins).

on the big and small screen convinced us that a movie musical *can* connect with audiences. But when you bring a stage piece to film, you have to analyze the bones of the material and translate it into a language that will speak to a filmgoing audience. Things that work on stage often don't translate well.

The movie must have its context in a world of heightened reality that we can understand. And this has to do with period, style and color palette. The world you create can't be too naturalistic, because if it's too authentic and real, it's very jarring when characters break into song and dance. So you have to aim for a slightly heightened reality. While we worked hard in *Hairspray* to make the characters extraordinarily human and real and to avoid anything self-conscious, we still needed to set those characters in a world that was a little exaggerated. They're not commenting on the sixties … yet they're not authentically of the sixties, either. The writer and director create rhythms in the action and dialogue that ramp up naturally to the moments when singing and dancing break out. All aspects of the production—script, direction, sets, costumes, cinematography—must work together to make this seem authentic. You can see this delicate blend of emotional realism and heightened reality in all the great movie musicals: the Kansas of *Wizard of Oz* and the Swiss Alps of *Sound of Music* are not quite real. But the characters' emotional journeys are, and both are worlds where you can believe people bursting into song.

It was always clear to us that *Hairspray* could be a memorable movie musical, if handled properly. It has rich and timeless themes that have connected with audiences since New Line released the original movie in 1988. As in our other movie musicals, the underlying theme is always an exploration of family: the eccentric yet deeply loving Turnblads, who grow and make new discoveries about each other during the story. The contrasting families like the Pingletons and Von Tussles. Motormouth Maybelle is the matriarch of a much larger family

Producers Zadan and Meron with John Travolta, as Edna Turnblad, in her fantasy flamenco costume for "Timeless to Me."

"We think of all the Hairspray progeny as sharing the same DNA. They're very much related to each other, yet each is an individual."
— *Producer Neil Meron*

that ends up taking in Tracy and her friends. The movie also has the eternal theme of the outsider, Tracy, who won't accept rejection, who dances her way onto center stage and ultimately brings everyone else around to her way of thinking. And then she realizes there's something even bigger—the goal of overcoming racial injustice, which needless to say is still with us.

These big themes give *Hairspray* a depth and universal appeal that we always look for in musicals, but they have to be woven into the fabric of an entertaining comedy. We relied on our screenwriter, Leslie Dixon, and our director-choreographer, Adam Shankman, to find and sustain the right comic tone from start to finish. When you do a musical for film, it's the most intense kind of collaboration, more so than with any other kind of movie. You need to have a cohesive vision with all your designers. Every element needs to work together, to achieve a singular look, the proper color palette. And again, to create a world where the characters can sing. People think that giant special effects movies, those huge logistical action movies, are complicated—it's nothing compared to doing a movie musical. There are so many moving parts.

And of course finding the right cast is paramount. To us, part of keeping the integrity of musicals alive is that the performers do their own singing and dancing. When we cast someone, we want the audience to know that they have those abilities, that it isn't being done with doubles or vocal assists. You want the audience to be comfortable in the fact that the people that they see on the screen can actually do it. And we've been very blessed to find people with those talents, from the legendary John Travolta, to actors like Michelle Pfeiffer and Chris Walken, who haven't been seen in these kinds of roles for a long time, to the amazing young performers in our cast. We're very proud of them all and grateful for their commitment, and we're thrilled that what you see in *Hairspray* is the talent of these individuals coming through.

Even with everything on your side, it's still a scary proposition. When a musical works, it looks effortless. You don't see the sweat, compared with other kinds of movies where you can see the work that goes into them. And musicals don't work halfway: either they succeed, or they don't. When a musical doesn't work, it's like a soufflé that just falls. That's what's so terrifying about it. The odds are against you. Hitting the target is so hard because it's so small. You have to be right, and that involves the whole gambit of the right script, the right tone, the right cast, the right director, the right choreographer, the right music.

We respond to musicals that move us on an emotional level. The greatest musicals are really about the human condition. And when you add the element of song to something that is charged, it only makes you feel more deeply about it. Some people have the idea that musicals are just happy and fun and have no substance. *Hairspray* is enormous fun, yet it has a great deal of underlying emotion. We hope people will walk away having been wildly entertained but also touched.

When they work, movie musicals bring a visceral reaction from an audience. When our movie of *Chicago* was in theaters, we'd go stand at the back of the theater, and at the end of the musical numbers people would applaud. You don't get that reaction to other types of movies. Music has that impact because it can penetrate like no other form. Music reaches people's souls in a way that drama or comedy alone do not.

Think about the great experiences you've had watching movie musicals—think of your emotional response to *Grease*, or to *The Wizard Of Oz, The Sound Of Music, West Side Story, Cabaret*. You cannot match that experience with another genre. Children remember their first brush with *Mary Poppins* or *Chitty-Chitty Bang-Bang*. These are powerful responses.

Hopefully *Hairspray* will join that list.

Dear Audience

by Adam Shankman

To say that making *Hairspray* was the single most fulfilling, enjoyable, emotionally draining and painfully fun experience I have known in my life would be an understatement of the grossest kind. Making movies is difficult, tedious and, frankly, for the criminally self-abusive. The hours, the politics, the judgments, the frustrations (and that's just picking locations!) are simply built in. Yet in every way, the happiness I experienced in making *Hairspray* overshadowed anything difficult or any negative feelings I ever had during its creation. Period.

Once upon a time, a frustrated chorus boy (me) fell in love with a fantastically mesmerizing movie called *Hairspray*, made by a singularly visionary filmmaker named John Waters. Divine, Rikki Lake, Deborah Harry, Jerry Stiller, Sonny Bono and Ruth Brown, to name just a few of its fantastic cast, bouncing around 1960s Baltimore, celebrating plus-size pleasures and race relations—all set to the most amazing music and choreographed to the teeth by the indelible Edward Love. I still think the scene where you first see the black kids dancing at Maybelle's may be one of my favorites ever.

It was a brilliant movie, full of the most grotesque humor (see: Amber's zit), the strangest tangential performances (see: Ric Ocasek and Pia Zadora), the best music ("Town Without Pity"), and the most beautiful message I'd ever seen. We are all equal and beautiful in our own way, so celebrate it all. How'd he do that??? I watched it over and over again, not realizing what an important gift I was receiving, because the wrapping paper was so insane.

Many years later, two of my best friends, Marc Shaiman and Scott Wittman, told me over a game of

Scrabble that they'd begun writing music and lyrics for a Broadway workshop production of *Hairspray*. Rob Marshall would be directing and choreographing. Harvey Fierstein would be starring—and I would be seething with jealousy in a corner. It was like somebody was dreaming my own dream instead of me, and I was outside the thought bubble banging on the fuzzy, cloudy stuff that encases dreams, screaming to get in, and no one would listen. This could be said of most of my life, but that's a foreword for a different coffee-table book. A scary one with a lot of swear words and tear-stained pages in it … but I digress.

I first saw *Hairspray the Musical* in its out-of-town tryouts in Seattle. By this time, Jack O'Brien and Jerry Mitchell had replaced Rob Marshall (who was off directing the movie of *Chicago*). It was dazzling. True to my friends' predictions, I seethed with jealousy in a corner of the theater, as the audience virtually tore their seats out of the floor and ate them by the time the finale anthem, "You Can't Stop the Beat," came to its conclusion. It was a smash on Broadway and went on to win a bazillion Tonys, including Best Musical of the year, which it was. Even one for my friend Marc, the five-time Oscar loser. I, the one-time Oscars dancer, loved it. I wanted to eat it, I loved it so much. All I wanted was somehow to be a part of it.

Fast-forward a few more years: Due to a scheduling conflict, Jack and Jerry became unable to work on the movie version of their megahit, and the movie gods (that would be the New Line brass) smiled upon me. I got the job. What tickled me most was that I would be doing double duty as choreographer *and* director. As Jerry Stiller, Mr. Pinky in the movie, so aptly puts it: "I hit the mother lode!!" I was beside myself with joy, a yoga

> *"I always knew that in the brain of this movie, music and dancing should be going on constantly—because that's what Tracy has going on in her head constantly. If I weren't a choreographer, I wouldn't have understood what it is to want to dance that badly."*
>
> — *Adam Shankman*

position I don't recommend to nondancers out there. I can't thank producers Craig Zadan and Neil Meron enough for their support.

And then the torch pass of all time happened! John Waters took me to lunch in Baltimore and showed me the streets where the action really took place and the homes of the people whom the characters were based on. I was in heaven. I hope very much that John is proud of his chubby grandchild: this movie. I thought of him every day in a "What would John do?" kind of way.

I would go on to team up with my best friends, associate choreographer Anne Fletcher and line producer Garrett Grant, my sister and partner l'il Jenny Gibgot, as well as Marc and Scott and a pack of great design talents—and, like Mickey Rooney and Judy Garland, put on a show. This one, amazingly, would star John Travolta, Michelle Pfeiffer, Queen Latifah, Christopher Walken, James Marsden, Allison Janney, Elijah Kelley, Zac Efron, Amanda Bynes, Brittany Snow, and our remarkable newbie, the outrageously talented teenager Nikki Blonsky, who worked in a Coldstone Creamery and auditioned via MySpace. Life is weird. *Hairspray* is weirder.

If you want to know all the dirt on production, you'll just have to keep reading this book. Or better yet, buy the DVD and listen to the director's commentary. (How's that for a plug?) For now, suffice to say it was a magical time spent in an upside-down world. All I wanted to do was maintain the indomitable spirit, energy and exuberance of the play and merge it with John Waters's rebellious and anarchistic sensibility. I did the best I could with what I had. Now it's all yours. My baby left the nest. I hope you love it as I do, and remember: We are all equal and beautiful in our own ways. Celebrate it every day.

P.S. Thank you, David James, for the amazing pictures. You are a true artist.

These pages: Director-choreographer Adam Shankman at work on the set. Top: Sharing a laugh with Nikki Blonsky (Tracy Turnblad). Above: With a vintage TV camera used on The Corny Collins Show.

Mama Edna's Turn

by John Travolta

When I was approached about *Hairspray*, my first impulse was to say no, as I've been saying for many years when someone asks me to consider a musical. There are so few that really work, and you have to be careful in making choices because you can get egg on your face pretty quickly. I felt like I had set a standard for myself a long time ago, with *Grease*—and the fact that it's still around 30 years later, and still plays to audiences of all ages, is a point of pride for me.

But the producers, Craig Zadan and Neil Meron, had a great track record, and Adam Shankman had a very clear vision of what he wanted to do. So when I said, tell me why *Hairspray* is going to work, they had good answers. Sometimes you just have an instinct when you meet with people, a gut reaction that they know what they're doing. Of course, that doesn't mean that your job's over. It's just beginning because you have to put your own signature on the project.

Playing Edna presented a lot of challenges, the first being that it had been done brilliantly twice before. Thinking about how I might interpret her, I had to think about what would be right for this movie and how that would be different from what Divine and Harvey Fierstein did. In both cases, it was basically a man playing a woman and everyone knows it, in the honorable drag tradition that's been done since vaudeville. But why try to compete with something that's been done so well already? Besides, playing the joke of the deep voice and the beard showing through didn't seem right for this movie, which was aiming for more realism overall. I knew that a lot could be done with prosthetics, and I thought it would be funnier for audiences to wonder how that could possibly be John Travolta under those big breasts and that big ass?

Mainly I wanted to be convincing as a woman, as Edna, through acting. I started to have an idea of who this Edna was, and therefore how I'd play her. I thought that in her day— before she put on all the weight—she was a hot tamale. The kind of woman that could have torn you up. Very voluptuous and flirtatious, and a little coy. But after she had her little girl, she let herself go, and once she got so heavy, she was embarrassed to be seen in public. I saw her as a

kind of Sophia Loren or Anita Eckberg gone to flesh, a real sexy woman who'd just gone south with her weight.

After a while, she just stops going out of the house at all. She rationalizes that she has her laundry business to run, and Tracy and Wilbur to take care of. So she starts out in this place of being trapped and treading on her daughter's dreams, but then Tracy inspires her to change. Once Tracy drags her out of the house, Edna starts to see some hope and possibilities for herself out there. Instead of being afraid of black people, she can warm up to Motormouth Maybelle, because they're not that different. She's negotiating deals with Mr. Pinky, and later in that scene she gets goosed up in pink glitz and goes into a big dance number. It's a tribute to the filmmakers that this all seems very natural, moving easily from dialogue into song, a lot like *Grease* did.

My characterization of Edna came partly from her relationship with her daughter and from knowing that Edna would be singing and dancing a lot in this movie. Because Tracy turns out to be such a good dancer, it makes sense that her mom would be, too, with a little encouragement. Why wouldn't Tracy be a chip off the old block? All the singing and dancing really reshapes the core of the character. Of course they hired me because I could do those things, so why not take advantage of it? But the character arc had to encompass the idea that she was really something back when—so when she comes out of her shell, she really busts out. And I got to have more fun portraying it this way.

I'm lucky that I can sing in a fairly high register, so that helped with my feminine take on Edna. And I wanted to do a Baltimore accent, which is such a fun and unique accent, and also makes you speak in a higher register, way up there. I knew enough people from Baltimore to have the basic idea but also had an expert coach, Robert Eastman, who ran through the script with me so I would get it right. I think it really helps communicate the character and the story. It's funny, it says blue collar, and the cadences are hilarious.

The special makeup also affected how the character turned out. Tony Gardner and his team went through so many different versions of the facial

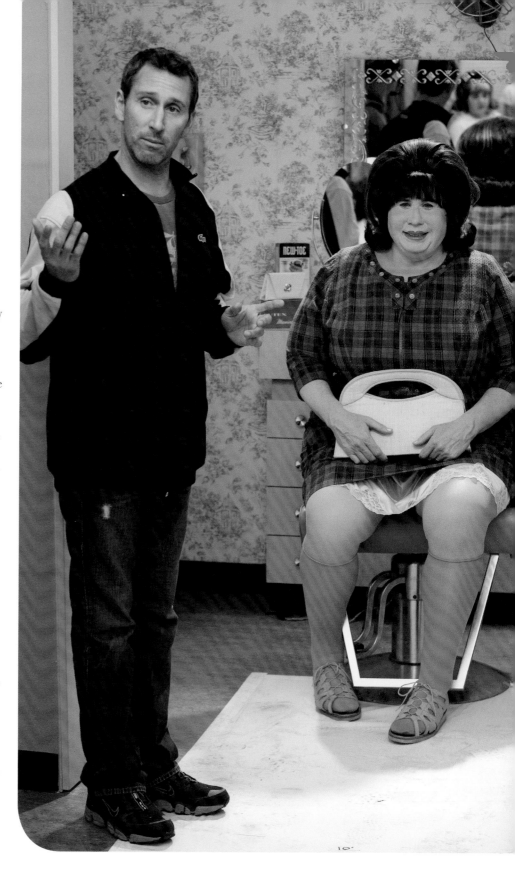

"Every day the guys on the set would forget that it was me underneath all the prosthetics. They'd go, 'How you doin', Edna?' And they'd flirt."

— *John Travolta*

prosthetics and wigs that I was never sure how it would end up. When it all got done, it was magical: I put on a nightgown, went in for the screen test, and smiled this big cheesy smile that had seven layers of chin, and big cheeks and all that. And out of nowhere, Edna suddenly lived. She came out kind of bubbly, more like a sister to Tracy than a mother, though she has lots of motherly qualities. Once he saw it, Adam encouraged me to play her that way. And it was a bonus that Nikki, who plays Tracy, even looked like me in my Edna makeup— our smiles and joie de vivre, even our movements look similar. That was partly intuitive and partly choreography, but when you see us in the number "Welcome to the Sixties" we look genetically connected.

The changes Edna goes through are reflected in her costumes too. I thought her clothing shouldn't be too flamboyant, especially at the beginning. Let's make her lower-middle-class Baltimore, downtrodden—in duller colors—then build as we go. Again I went to pictures of Sophia Loren, who always dressed in a very low-key way, so you didn't care about the clothes, you cared about her. Then later, in the big, bright "Welcome to the Sixties" number we go to pink sequins, and by the finale Edna's in red.

Edna's way of moving was probably the easiest thing for me, because once I know how a character walks or dances, I can come up with organic moves. The prosthetics were somewhat limiting, but as a dancer you can put a layer under those layers that makes something funny or sensuous or whatever. You've made a myriad of decisions about softening the edges, letting wrists go limp and fingers flow and legs kick and head go back. You can turn her into a dancing woman, and just forget all the masculine qualities. It's a state of mind. Just like, if you're Danny Zucko, you're dancing like Elvis Presley, or if you're the archangel Michael [in the film of the same name], you're using what he brings to his dancing from throughout the ages.

The big finale is where Edna really breaks loose in front of a crowd. I wanted her to be defined as a performer in that moment especially. And my inspiration for a performer with great female energy was Tina Turner. So Adam worked up a dance break for Edna in that number that looks like something Tina might have done. It's Edna's big moment — like in *Gypsy*, where the mother sings "Rose's Turn." Only this is Mama Edna's Turn. It's a spectacular number, and I like to think that, after all these years, she finally understands why Tracy loves to dance more than anything.

From Screen to Stage to Screen

Since *The Desert Song* in 1929, people have been adapting successful Broadway musicals into movie musicals. We grew up with them: *South Pacific, West Side Story, The Sound of Music, Grease,* and scores of others. But there's a much smaller list of movie musicals that started life as another kind of movie … then were transformed into musicals … and finally made the journey back to the big screen. Joining that list now is *Hairspray.*

It takes a special story to have the legs for this journey. There's no question that *Hairspray* has been a bright star in the entertainment universe almost since the day John Waters's original movie opened in 1988. Its devotees included this film's director, Adam Shankman. "I'm a huge fan of the Broadway play. And I watched the John Waters movie religiously when I was younger. It still holds up for me—it's a really funny, arch, anarchistic movie that is actually about something."

Beyond that, the stars have to be aligned perfectly for a movie musical to be born. For *Hairspray* this meant a progenitor who was glad to see his brainchild adopted by other branches of the entertainment family: Waters became a benevolent godfather to both the musical and the new movie. It meant visionary producers Craig Zadan and Neil Meron, Tony Award-winning songwriters Marc Shaiman and Scott Wittman, and hit filmmaker-director-choreographer Adam Shankman. It meant a pioneering studio, New Line Cinema, with a big stake in all three properties, and an all-star cast who wanted to be part of the *Hairspray* legend and the movie musicals revival. And maybe not least, a culture that seems perennially hungry for the spirit, sounds and messages *Hairspray* has delivered in each of its appearances—hungry for the last innocent time Americans can remember, and the music we remember it by.

Hairspray's Roots

"John Waters has been so remarkable," says producer Craig Zadan. "He gave us the most important gift. When they were doing the Broadway musical, he told them: do your thing. Just create a Broadway show that works for you. And he said the same thing to us: Don't copy my movie, don't copy their Broadway musical. Do your movie musical of *Hairspray,* and do what you

need to make it great. So he basically liberated all of us. We were able to invent and know that we had his blessing, which was very important to us. Because he's the father of this story and these characters."

The first *Hairspray* was conceived in John Waters's old apartment in Baltimore in the early 1980s. The Baltimore homeboy was already famous—some might say notorious—for the low-budget films he had made beginning in the late 1960s with an ensemble of local actors: films that pushed cinematic

Producers Zadan and Meron with John Waters on the Baltimore set in Toronto.

boundaries by exploring the margins of society and sexuality. Best-known among these were *Pink Flamingoes, Female Trouble,* and *Desperate Living,* which Waters called his "Trash Trilogy." All these films, and more in the Waters oeuvre, were released by a maverick young studio, New Line Cinema. And the most of them featured Waters's close friend and collaborator: a fearless drag actor known as Divine. Both relationships would be vital to the success of *Hairspray.*

The idea for *Hairspray* sprang from Waters's youthful passion for a Baltimore

Above, left to right: Baltimore dance show host Buddy Deane, Divine as the original Edna, and Ricki Lake as Tracy.

TV dance program called *The Buddy Deane Show*, which aired from 1957 to 1964 and was phenomenally successful. Waters recalls, "While the rest of the nation grew up on Dick Clark's *American Bandstand* … Baltimoreans, true to form, had their own eccentric version. Every rock 'n' roll star of the day (except Elvis) came to town to lip-synch and plug their records on the show: Buddy Holly, Bill Haley, Fats Domino, the Supremes, Annette Funicello, Frankie Avalon, and Fabian, to name just a few.

"You learned how to be a teenager from the show," says Waters. "Every day after school kids would run home, tune in, and dance with the bedpost or refrigerator door as they watched." That image will be recognized by any fan of *Hairspray*, whose early scenes show Tracy Turnblad and her friend Penny racing home to catch *The Corny Collins Show*—Waters's film version of the Deane show.

Hairspray's irrepressible heroine, Tracy Turnblad, had her prototype in a popular 14-year-old regular on the Deane show. Waters put some of himself in the Tracy character too: he was the striver who could never crack the ranks of the show's regular dancers. And the movie's deeper theme arose from the hard fact that the show—though it celebrated the music of black recording artists and set aside occasional days for black kids to come and dance—would never allow black and white kids to dance together on the show. As Scott Wittman put it, "John wanted to make a comedy about racial tension but with a happy ending."

Divine starred in the now-classic role of Edna Turnblad, Tracy's mom, joined by other members of Waters's usual company, including Mink Stole. The writer-director also looked beyond Baltimore for his cast: to mainstream actors like Jerry Stiller (Wilbur Turnblad), entertainment figures like Sonny Bono and Debbie Harry, and a college girl, Ricki Lake, who became the first of several unknowns to play Tracy. Made for a budget of about $2 million, entirely on location in Baltimore and a nearby Pennsylvania amusement park, *Hairspray* (1988) was permeated with John Waters's blithely transgressive comic spirit. After a surprisingly strong opening weekend, it went on to become a sleeper hit for New Line, with an even stronger (and apparently endless) life on home video to follow. For Waters and his cast, though, its success was bittersweet: Divine died in her sleep just a few days after the film opened and never got to enjoy her mainstream stardom.

"I think everybody relates to the story," says Leslie Dixon, who wrote the screenplay for the movie musical. "Everybody relates to John Waters's original concept of this underdog heroine who thinks she can do anything. And I was a huge fan of the musical, too, knew the whole score—like a whole lot of people."

There are various tales of how *Hairspray the Musical* came about, but they all start in 2001 with respected Broadway producer Margo Lion (*Angels in America*) at home with the flu and a stack of videos—one of which was *Hairspray*. (Theatrical rights actually had been optioned by producer Scott Rudin almost a decade earlier, but that project never got off the ground.) Struck with its potential for the musical stage, Lion persuaded New Line and other investors that she was the right person to produce the adaptation, then set about putting together a creative team.

At her side was Mark Kaufman, who had been New Line's man on the scene since the beginning. "I'd had a long relationship with John Waters; I used to clear music for his movies," says Kaufman. He became the production executive for the 1988 film; then was assigned as New Line's liaison to supervise production of the musical. "I became Margo Lion's shadow, from creation to casting to tryouts and the eventual Broadway opening," he notes. Now executive VP for production and development for New Line, he's overseeing *Hairspray* 2007. "Watching the whole thing unfold has been extraordinary."

Songs make the musical, so the choice of composer and lyricist was step one. And *Hairspray* presented a special challenge. As Marc Shaiman, the show's composer and co-lyricist with his partner, Scott Wittman, explains: "Writing songs for *Hairspray* was like walking a tightrope. We had to balance the traditional Broadway song style, with its tight narrative, perfect rhymes, and precise rhythms, with the pop vernacular of the early sixties."

Shaiman and Wittman had co-written off-Broadway shows in earlier years, but their reputation was chiefly for work in movies: Shaiman's credits include several Oscar-nominated scores and songs (most recently for *South Park: Bigger, Longer, Uncut*). "I was doing one movie score after another and was really ready for something different," says Shaiman. "We were starting to feel like Broadway had passed us by. We had done smaller shows in the eighties but then came that long spate of Andrew Lloyd Webber and other shows in a more

Left: Harvey Fierstein as Divine, Marissa Jaret Winokur as Tracy, Matthew Morrison as Link, Dick Latessa as Wilbur Turnblad. Photo by Paul Kolnik.

"These filmmakers understand the humor and what my movie and the musical were about. Adam Shankman and I drove all around Baltimore, the real neighborhoods where it happened, and we had a great time. I think Adam really has the right ideas about the story."
— *John Waters*

bombastic vein. *Hairspray* was right up our street, so I couldn't let this chance go by."

The team wrote four songs on spec, demonstrating that they were more than up to the task. "We were lucky," Shaiman believes, "because that period was full of dramatic stories told in pop songs, probably more than any other era. You think of story songs like "Leader of the Pack" or Leslie Gore's "It's My Party" or anything by the Shangri-Las. Those were our model for *Hairspray*. It was a great way into the songwriting."

Neil Meron, co-producer with Zadan of the movie musical, marvels at the rich score created by Shaiman and Wittman. "They're a great songwriting team who understands the genre. They take a period, like 1962, and write what sound like very authentic songs of the era. They can do the rock 'n' roll sound of a Chubby Checker. They can capture the girl group sound, an Elvis Presley type of sound, rumbas and sambas, and then do their own take on these genres. The songs aren't copies; these are really fresh songs."

Most of the songs written for the Broadway show are heard in the movie musical as well, providing, as Meron says, "the pulsing drive of music throughout the entire film. The constant music lets you feel the era and have a great time. It's feel-good music. And the songs help you understand the characters. Their cleverness brought out different levels of each character."

Meron and Zadan saw the musical more than once when making plans for their film. Adds Zadan: "Sitting in that Broadway theater, you observed that the show created such a frenzied momentum that by the time you got to the end, you literally watched people wanting to dance in the aisles. You were completely jazzed because they created this magical journey through the music."

Once the songwriters were at work, says Shaiman, "Margo allowed us to become the engine, while she kept matchmaking." After several tries, Mark O'Donnell and Thomas Meehan were hired to write the show's book, creating dialogue that would mesh perfectly with the songs. Recruiting the show's production staff and casting the roles brought more great talent to the project, convincing everyone that *Hairspray the Musical* was blessed. An early collaborator while the show was in workshops was director-choreographer Rob Marshall, the creative force behind the Oscar-winning *Chicago*. After Marshall left to direct that landmark movie musical, a new team of director

Jack O'Brien and choreographer Jerry Mitchell took over, shaping and guiding the show through tryouts and the Broadway opening.

In the most inspired piece of casting since Divine, the inimitable Harvey Fierstein was awarded the role of Edna, continuing the tradition that the role is played by a male actor. Another tradition—of a very young, plus-size, unknown actress playing Tracy—was fulfilled by the delightful Marissa Jaret Winokur. The rest of the ensemble drawn from Broadway's rich talent pool not only made the show sparkle but melded into a close-knit family backstage. Shaiman and Wittman credit this to "that *Hairspray* spirit of happiness."

The musical had its tryout run in Seattle to packed and pumped houses. "We knew we had something special then," notes Mark Kaufman. After a few tweaks, the show opened on Broadway in August 2002 to rave reviews, and audiences have been flocking to it ever since. One reason, the creators believe, was New Yorkers' need for a few hours of nostalgic respite among the ruins of 9/11. Says Kaufman: "I think we developed a special relationship with audiences because of that. The show soothed people; it became a place they went to be cheered and comforted, a brief escape into a more innocent world." But *Hairspray* had other special qualities, too, as it proved by winning eight Tony Awards in 2003, including Best Musical.

A Movie Musical Is Born

With famous ancestors like the Waters movie and the play, *Hairspray* the movie musical has a lot to live up to. Not that this deterred the filmmakers: after all, they had great bloodlines to work with. "We think of all the *Hairspray* progeny as sharing the same DNA," says Neil Meron. "They're very much related to each other, yet each is an individual. The creators of the Broadway musical brought their originality and energy and point of view to what they did on stage. As the creators of the film musical have done now."

A few years into the show's run on Broadway, executives at New Line began to discuss bringing the musical to the screen. "*Chicago* had opened the door to doing more movie musicals and shown they could be successful," says Mark Kaufman. New Line had no plans to part with this valuable property, so the studio began hunting for the right team to produce, write, and direct a new

Right: Adam Shankman with Nikki Blonsky.

film. One thing they knew for sure: "We didn't want it to be just a souvenir version of *Hairspray the Musical*," says Kaufman. "We hoped the two versions would be complementary, each drawing new audiences for the other. We thought the story could be reimagined in a way slightly closer to the original film, with the social justice theme developed more than you could on stage."

Now as before, the right people found *Hairspray*. Among the star-studded audience at one of the musical's last previews were producers Craig Zadan and Neil Meron. Their just-completed movie of *Chicago* was in post-production, to be released that December. They were looking for a new project. "When we saw *Hairspray*, we thought it would make an incredible movie musical," recalls Meron. "And a great follow-up to *Chicago* for us because it's completely different in tone."

"We fell madly in love with *Hairspray*," agrees Zadan. "We knew that eventually it would be made into a movie ... then we saw an announcement that it was going forward." At that point, Zadan and Meron began seriously wooing the musical's creators as well as New Line. They had dinner with songwriters Shaiman and Wittman, and the show's director and choreographer, Jack O'Brien and Jerry Mitchell, to explain their way of bringing musicals to the screen. *Chicago* was the most recent, but their experience reached back to 1993 with the successful TV production of *Gypsy*, followed later on TV by Rodgers & Hammerstein's *Cinderella*, then by *Annie*.

The producers essentially "auditioned" for New Line, meeting first in New York with Mark Kaufman, then on the West Coast with studio president Toby Emmerich, "to tell them our point of view and bring them through how we do our movie musicals," says Meron. "People wondered: why are you auditioning? You've just done *Chicago*, the first movie musical in 34 years to win the Oscar for Best Picture," Zadan recalls. "But it was because we wanted to do it so much. Like when an actor says, I'm going to do whatever it takes to get that part. We'd do anything necessary to show that we were the right people to produce this movie."

Zadan and Meron's ideas about how to do *Hairspray* were completely in synch with New Line's hopes. They firmly intended to make a movie that shared the same roots and spirit as the 1988 film and the musical but stood on its own. "The sense of collaboration we got from New Line has been probably our best experience with a studio," says Meron. "It's known as a maverick company for good reason—because they take chances. They're creatively astute, and they like to play with the rules a bit, which is important when you're approaching a movie musical like *Hairspray*."

Bringing in the Translators

Reshaping the material from film to stage and then back to a film musical is a process that requires skilled translation, says Neil Meron. "Because each form has its own language. You have to find the language that can speak in the medium you're producing. Here, the translators were our screenwriter and our director, who could envision the Broadway musical in a film world."

The first key decision by New Line and the producers was to bring in screenwriter Leslie Dixon to reshape the story. Dixon's credits included *Outrageous Fortune* and a critical rewrite on *Mrs. Doubtfire*. "Tonally, we felt that her writing was in the direction we wanted to go with *Hairspray*," says Meron. "She's been able in her movies to create comic characters that are still very real."

Not just tone but content and pacing had to be recalibrated. In some cases, Dixon would recreate or reinvent a scene from the Broadway show. But mostly she wrote new scenes that weren't in the musical, based on something a character might do or how a situation might play out—"loving the source

Left: The cast of The Corny Collins Show.

"Everybody relates to John Waters's original concept of this underdog heroine who thinks she can do anything."
— *Screenwriter Leslie Dixon*

material and yet not being religious about it," as Meron puts it.

"Movies are more literal than the stage," Zadan observes. "You have to plot out the story more than in a stage show, where you can just be dazzled by the singing and dancing and how much fun it all is. On stage, you don't stop to question how a bunch of characters suddenly find themselves in a certain place. But when you're putting a movie together, you have to work through all those issues. People pay attention to logic and continuity and causality: how do all these people get there? And how does this resolve?"

Changes in the script also brought changes to the music. This was delicate, as fans get very attached to songs, but they couldn't be sacrosanct. A few songs had to be cut because they didn't work on film; conversely, new elements in the screenplay called for "musicalization." Shaiman and Whitman worked with the filmmakers to write new songs for the production. "Adding songs was never gratuitous," says Meron. "It was always from realizing that a moment needed musical expression."

Even songs that were imported from stage to screen had to be treated differently in the new environment. "We knew that the audience will not sit still for scenes that go on and on in the same location," says Dixon. "In a Broadway show you can have maybe three musical numbers in a row in one location. Movie audiences aren't going to sit in their seats for 15 minutes while people sing three songs on the same soundstage."

The songs were cut up to make the action move from place to place within the framework of a musical number. "No sequence remains in the same location for more than three or four minutes without cutting away to something," Dixon says. "Or the number itself moves to another place: outside, or into another room, onto a bus— something to make it feel like a movie and not a filmed play."

The producers and director give Dixon high points for her creative

contribution. "When we got Leslie's script, we were sort of overjoyed," says Zadan. "Because she had made the characters much more full-bodied." The script became very important in attracting the cast they wanted, because sometimes when people saw the Broadway show, they didn't immediately understand how it could become a movie. But, says Meron, "when we sent that script out to actors, instead of them saying, I don't get it, they got it right away."

What went into the movie and how it would be realized on screen began with the script but very soon had to involve the director and choreographer. They would bring their own visions of how the action and characterizations would unfold, how the musical numbers would be woven in. New Line originally hired the Broadway team of director Jack O'Brien and choreographer Jerry Mitchell. But because of the inevitable time lag between early planning and final production, both became unavailable due to prior stage commitments. This left the challenge of hiring anew for those two key posts.

First, the director: finding someone with a deep understanding of film, music, and dance, who could effectively lead and manage the enormous production. They spoke with more than a dozen candidates over about three months of interviews—long-established as well as younger directors. Many wanted the job, but none seemed to fill the bill exactly. Until the producers sat down with a director who already had helmed several commercial hit movies: Adam Shankman.

Not only was Shankman a noted expert in contemporary comedy (*The Wedding Planner, Bringing Down the House*), but he also brought a résumé no other director possessed. "What people didn't know about Adam is that he started off as a dancer, and then became a prominent choreographer for film," says Neil Meron. "He had choreographed musical sequences in dozens of movies before he turned into one of Hollywood's most successful directors yet had never done a movie musical."

It was instantly clear that having a director and choreographer in one body and mind would be a huge advantage for *Hairspray*. "The true director-choreographer is so ideal for a movie musical," notes Meron. "It's about timing and movement and being able to see things from a choreographic point of view. And it's so rare you get all that in one package."

"When we looked at the choices," adds Zadan, "the only person that made

Above: Adam Shankman with director of photography Bojan Bazelli, and Elijah Kelley (Seaweed) and dancers. Below: Shankman and Fletcher rehearse the "Detention Kids."

sense to us on every conceivable level was Adam. In our preliminary meetings, he said everything that we were feeling. He understood the script and where it needed to go. Sets, costumes … we were in sync on every item." Meron concurs. "Adam had such an amazing passion to do this. To him, this is not just an assignment; it's more of a mission. I think he feels a great responsibility to tell this story in a deeply emotional and funny way."

Shankman's work with the script, the production crew, the actors and dancers, all bore out their hopes. "Adam's remarkable achievement has been to find a comedic tone that allows these deeply unconventional characters to exist and the audience to relate to them," Meron states. "He goes right up to the edge of comic sensibility but always pulls back enough to show the heart." Adds Zadan, "He knows how to direct comedy. He knows where the funny is. And *Hairspray* is an entertainment above all else."

For Shankman, the assignment united his background, his love of the sources, and his most cherished ambitions. Directing a movie musical was a chance he hoped—but was never certain—would come. "I'm a chorus boy. I was a dancer," he recounts. "I did a lot of musicals since I was a little kid. So making a musical was certainly something I always wished for. And the prayers got answered."

That dance background guided all his important choices on the film, he says. "I always knew that in the brain of this movie, music and dancing should be going on constantly—because that's what Tracy has going on in her head constantly. In trying to see the whole story through Tracy's eyes, I recognized that what she wants to do is dance. If I weren't a choreographer, I wouldn't have understood what it is to want to dance that badly."

Shankman was thrilled to work with longtime friends Marc Shaiman and Scott Wittman, a happy coincidence. And as a fan, he appreciated the chance to build on John Waters's legacy, his daring blend of the silly and sober: "*Hairspray* isn't just about family or achieving your dreams. It's about changing history and seeing everyone beyond skin color."

Shankman worked closely with Leslie Dixon, his collaborator previously on *Bringing Down the House*, to incorporate his insights into the story development. He was sensitive to anything that seemed too broadly comic. "I think you can't do broad, and then bring in songs like 'I Know Where I've Been.' It's too jarring. And when Link abandons Tracy and she's all alone in the bomb shelter, I want your heart to break for her. You can't do broad against that," he says. "So I tried to make the comedy more sophisticated."

The musical numbers as originally scripted had to be rethought as well, says Shankman. "I saw the numbers in my head very early on, and I wanted to approach them more dramatically rather than from a simple dancing/staging perspective."

The keys to making a musical film, says Shankman, include "trying to make interesting images that go with the numbers, creating a heightened world, and managing the transitions from speech into musical number." Especially important, he felt, was that the first time you hear a character sing, it has to make sense to the audience. "Again, the trick was how Tracy never stops hearing music in her head. She wakes up, and the music is already going. So once we get into 'Good Morning, Baltimore,' I think and hope that audiences will buy it right off the bat, because Tracy buys it."

He and Dixon worked to make sure the film story didn't gloss over any important details of plot logic. "Like getting all the characters to Maybelle's store at the end of act one, or getting everyone into the Miss Teenage Hairspray Pageant. We paid a lot of attention to making sure all those holes were filled, and that the plot tracked in a linear, logical and hopefully interesting way. We also tried to take numbers that were static on the stage and make them more visually arresting. Like attaching the Maybelle song 'I Know Where I've Been' to a protest march."

In all, he calls the project a life-changing experience. "To do a comedy with

John Travolta as Edna, with Nikki Blonsky (left) and recording one of his songs (center).

a message like this, to stage and interpret these wonderful songs, and to put so much dance into it—this movie's just a revelation for me personally. I made way more dancing than exists even in the play. Because of the nature of the music and subject matter, the choreography just kind of poured out of me—maybe because I hadn't choreographed in a long time.

"*Hairspray* is nothing if not a celebration," he concludes, "and I hope audiences take that away."

Actors, Singing and Dancing

Film characterizations come from many sources: the director has definite ideas, and the material itself is primary. Notes Shankman, "There are lines in the songs and lines in the script that give you little clues as to who the characters are"—in particular the Turnblad family members and their relationships. But the X factor that sparks a film is what the actors bring.

"When you do movie musicals, casting is key," confirms Neil Meron. "Because you want the words to come alive. And you want there to be surprises. We look for little twists that will make the project better, that will elevate it."

Casting *Hairspray* was like a huge puzzle with many moving parts, from the principal leads to the several hundred dancers and hundreds more extras. And the filmmakers introduced another degree of difficulty, a factor they insist is crucial to making movie musicals work today. They had to find stars who could not only portray the characters with conviction but could pull off the serious singing and dancing required.

Veteran casting directors David Rubin and Richard Hicks were charged with coordinating this quest. "We were all determined to find actors that had the musical chops, the dancing chops, but fundamentally the acting chops so they could create the characters in a musical world," says Rubin. "Audiences now are not used to seeing characters sing, and the only way it works is if there's real integrity behind the character. You have to find someone who can be tremendously truthful and invested, and yet inevitably break into song. And it's a level of performance the stage show might not require because it's so in your face."

An inspired stroke of casting can set the tone for a production. At the producers' first meeting with New Line the question came up: Who would you cast as Edna Turnblad? "We had already talked about it," says Meron. "So we immediately said: John Travolta. It hadn't occurred to them till then, though New Line had already put together a laundry list of Hollywood's best.

"It just struck us that if John played Edna, it would elevate the project from a movie musical into an event. It would make the movie extra special. Once the idea had been voiced, it caught fire. And we spent the next year talking to John on and off about why he should take the role."

Travolta wanted to be sure that if he was going to do a movie musical at this point in his career, it would be a new high-water mark for him, says Craig Zadan. He was concerned that audiences associated him with song-and-dance roles he had played as a much younger man, in *Grease* and *Saturday Night Fever*. "We convinced him that if he didn't want to be compared to himself 30 years ago, this was a great choice. He wouldn't be playing anyone close to the roles in his earlier movies. And one of his career trademarks has been surprising the audience."

Travolta playing a woman would be a distinct surprise. And carrying on a tradition of male actors portraying Edna—beginning with Divine and continuing with Harvey Fierstein in the musical—would clearly be the acting stretch of a lifetime. It all made sense to the actor, who threw himself wholeheartedly into the job of putting his own signature on the character.

"I had turned down several movie musicals over the years, including Craig and Neil's *Chicago*, because I was busy doing other things, or I couldn't see how they would work," says Travolta. "But having watched the genre become more successful again, I thought I should at least meet with the producers and director and find out why they thought *Hairspray* would be different."

The actor gives full credit to all those who had a hand in his portrayal: the producers, the director and associate choreographers, his vocal coach, and the designers who created costumes, hairstyles, and special makeup to achieve his physical transformation into Edna. Being sheathed in prosthetics every day, not to mention dancing in them, was grueling work, but, Travolta insists, "I had fun with it. Every day the guys on the set would forget that it was me

The Way of Edna

"We believe in tradition," declares producer Craig Zadan. "And so we never considered having Edna played by other than a male actor in this production, though it was suggested to us." For precedent, he cites a famous example of cross-gender casting: Mary Martin in the original musical of *Peter Pan*, which was created for her. Later the role was played by Sandy Duncan and Cathy Rigby, among others—but never by a boy. The producers wanted to acknowledge the validity and daring of those earlier incarnations of Edna by Divine and Harvey Fierstein. "Not only were the earlier Ednas brilliantly conceived by the actors, including a Tony Award–winning performance by Fierstein, but a man playing Edna points up something special about this story." *Hairspray's* theme of the outsider rising above society's expectations is embodied in the revolutionary act of a man becoming a female character. And just as *Peter Pan* (played by a woman) sends a message that physical courage and leadership aren't necessarily the property of boys, *Hairspray's* male casting of Edna implicitly asks: What is exclusively female about being vulnerable, a bit insecure, and devoted to your family?

"It was like school. You woke up every morning and went to one period after another: music rehearsal, dance rehearsal, scene rehearsal."

— John Travolta

Travolta as Edna with Christopher Walken as Wilbur Turnblad.

Queen Latifah (left) and Michelle Pfeiffer (below) during recording sessions.

underneath it all. They'd go, 'How you doin', Edna?' And they'd flirt. And I'm thinking: the power of a woman. This outfit is fake, but it's still making guys melt."

The spirit of surprise carried through the principal casting. To play Tracy's other parent, dad Wilbur, the filmmakers turned to Christopher Walken at the explicit request of his friend Travolta. At first glance, an actor famed for his dramatic portrayals of men on the edge might seem an odd choice for *Hairspray*'s good-humored joke-shop proprietor. But what's not well known is that Walken started his performing career singing and dancing in musicals.

"I never set out to be an actor," Walken says. "But I've been in show business since I was a little boy. As a kid, I was what they called a triple threat. That meant you could sing a little, dance a little, and you could memorize a line. So you were hirable. And I went from that to being a chorus boy. I did a lot of musicals— touring companies, summer stock."

Says Adam Shankman, "I gravitated to Walken because I knew he was a song-and-dance man. There were far too few of those of the proper age around. And because he's such an original actor and always brings an off-center performance, I thought he was a great fit."

The pairing of Travolta and Walken as Edna and Wilbur was crucial in getting audiences to buy into their on-screen relationship—one reason Travolta made his plea. "The actor playing Wilbur had to help John believe that he was a woman married to this guy. If not, John's task would have been even more daunting," notes Richard Hicks. "When you see Chris Walken look at Edna and convey that she is the love of his life, then the audience believes it."

Another star of great range, who hadn't been seen in film for some years, is Michelle Pfeiffer, who plays Velma Von Tussle, the villain of the piece in her dual identity as boss of the TV station WYZT and stage-mother-from-hell of Tracy's rival, Amber. Pfeiffer sang and danced in one of her first films, *Grease 2*, and sang while voicing a character in the animated *Prince of Egypt*, but more people probably remember her steamy rendition of "Makin' Whoopee" in *The Fabulous Baker Boys*. "But it's been a while," notes Rubin. "So this will be a revelation to audiences."

Adam Shankman was thrilled to land the former beauty queen to play the former "Miss Baltimore Crabs" in *Hairspray*. "Michelle's performance in *Batman* told me that she could really handle the physical as well as the comedic elements here. And she just bit into the character like she had lockjaw. She

didn't shy away from how horrible Velma is and plays her with great stylish energy. And she's funny. I think people will be really taken by her comedy."

One performer whose potent singing and acting will surprise no one is Queen Latifah as Motormouth Maybelle, the role originated by blues great Ruth Brown. "There was simply no one else we ever seriously considered for the part," says Craig Zadan. "It was a list of one." To begin with, the singer-actress had a great history with the filmmakers: she had co-starred in the Zadan/Meron-produced *Chicago* (for which she won an Oscar nomination) and also worked with Adam Shankman in his comedy hit *Bringing Down the House*. "Not only is she a powerhouse musically, but she's proven herself a dramatic actress of real credibility," says David Rubin. "Coming from a very gritty urban tradition, she first earned her cred with one segment of the audience, music fans, and then managed to expand the breadth of her appeal without compromising where she came from. And because this character is so much about holding onto your roots but broadening your reach, she was a perfect fit in that way."

The *Hairspray* family of actors spanned the generations with James Marsden (of *X-Men* and *Superman* fame), who plays the singing and dancing Corny Collins. The famous established actors served as role models and mentors for the brilliant younger cast members, who include Zac Efron (*High School Musical*) as Link Larson, Amanda Bynes (*She's the Man*) as Penny Pingleton, Brittany Snow (from *The Pacifier*) as Amber Von Tussle, and newcomer Elijah Kelley as Seaweed Stubbs.

"We wanted to find young actors who really were or looked as if they could be teenagers," says Hicks. "The camera picks up something about an adolescent kid that is irreplaceable." Other cast members were impressed by how well-trained and professional their young colleagues turned out to be. Says Travolta, "Each of them is more equipped to do this level of musical than most actors I knew when we were young. I mean, we were a select few. These guys are on their game."

And then there's Tracy, the fizz in the *Hairspray* ... the character without whom the story doesn't exist. As Rubin observes, "Without a Tracy, you fall for from the very first frame, you are really sunk." There was good reason to "cast young" for the roles around her, because when Nikki Blonsky won the part of Tracy, after a worldwide search, she was just 17. "From day one, we all

Right: Nikki Blonsky with Bojan Bazelli (center), Adam Shankman and line producer Garrett Grant. Below: Rehearsing for the high school record hop.

"I just kept going back to Nikki's audition tape. She made me laugh a lot."
— *Adam Shankman*

agreed that we would not accept a star, even if a star existed who could play Tracy," says Zadan. "We wanted Tracy to be an unknown, discovered by the film." The massive search encompassed open calls across the U.S. and Canada, England, and finally Australia. Websites were put up to advertise the part, and thousands of audition tapes poured into the casting directors' office. Promising candidates went through several stages of tryouts, and a small handful were screen-tested. The qualifications were daunting: "We had to find someone of a certain stature and a certain age," says Zadan. "Who could really sing and dance. Who could not only act but carry a movie opposite all these big stars."

More than a thousand girls were seen, but as months went by with the role still unfilled, the filmmakers' nervousness mounted. "What if we're deluding ourselves?" Zadan recalls thinking. "We have a start date, we have a great script, a great cast, everything ready to go. What happens if we don't find Tracy?" They almost didn't. Nikki Blonsky's tape got routed to the wrong office; only by luck did an assistant, Tyler Gillett, happen to view it, see something special, and send it on to Rubin and Hicks. After Nikki auditioned for them, for Adam Shankman, for the producers, and was then screen-tested, it was finally a done

deal. The girl who had performed only as an amateur, who held down a job scooping ice cream while attending high school, was suddenly The Girl in a major Hollywood movie musical.

Everyone had the right feeling about Nikki from the first. "I just kept going back to Nikki's audition tape," says Shankman. "She made me laugh a lot. She had incredible confidence, was very pretty, and had a lovable sexuality that is very Tracy." The choice became crystal clear, says Meron, "from the moment we saw the screen test. When you film someone and project it on the big screen, it tells you right away whether the person can really do it."

Shankman still marvels at how easily his youngest star moved into her place on center stage, surrounded by Hollywood legends. Another unexpected gift was that, in makeup and wigs, Blonsky and Travolta looked uncannily as if they could be blood relations. Beyond that, their performances synched beautifully. "I needed a mother/daughter relationship that was buyable so you could understand who Tracy was, and what her real family was," says the director. Neil Meron believes Blonksy and Travolta's relationship was cemented when they first met. "John arrived. Saw Nikki, opened his arms and said, 'Come to Mama.'"

Attention to detail, love of surprise, and respect for tradition carried through in casting even the smallest roles. The part of Prudy Pingleton, the uptight-verging-on-unhinged mother of Tracy's friend Penny, went to Allison Janney, an actress better known for serious drama (*West Wing*) but who plays comedy just as adeptly. And to honor John Waters and evoke the spirit of his original film, some of the original stars were cast in cameo roles—including Waters himself, who plays a flasher. "You see, I'm typecast," he laughs. "But I love that I'm here and what it says: basically that I approve of what's being done and you're going to like it." Also brought back for cameos were Ricki Lake, who was just as much an unknown as Blonsky when she became the first Tracy, and Jerry Stiller, beloved as the original Wilbur Turnblad, who here takes on the hilarious part of Mr. Pinky, proprietor of the Hefty Hideaway boutique.

To cast something as complex as *Hairspray*, Neil Meron says, "You have to play jigsaw puzzle in your mind, make sure the pieces all fit together." Now the last pieces were in place. The creators' instincts and hard work paid off, not just in the assembled talent but in an amazing chemistry that bubbled among them. They took special pride in how the cast came together with, as Marc Shaiman comments, "not a single role compromised by anyone's level of celebrity or obscurity."

The Music Men

"The story of this movie is in the songs," says Adam Shankman. "There's barely a five-minute stretch when there isn't music going on." The Broadway musical of *Hairspray* was an unprecedented hit thanks largely to its award-winning, infectious score by composer-lyricist Marc Shaiman and his partner, lyricist Scott Wittman. The filmmakers of *Hairspray* 2007 had the good fortune to have Shaiman and Wittman participating throughout the production, from the writing stage through the final orchestrations.

In creating their original score, the songwriters took inspiration from the wondrous sounds of mid-century American pop, from "movie" Elvis to R&B to beach music to Motown—but also from John Waters's movie, which was a formative experience for both. "A lot of lines from the movie stood out as inspiration for songs," says Wittman. Like 'Mama, welcome to the sixties!' Or when Tracy says, 'Now all Baltimore knows I'm big, blonde and beautiful.' Even though we put her words in Motormouth Maybelle's mouth because to us the line suggested a barrelhouse blues."

"Good Morning, Baltimore" came from even deeper in the songwriters' genetic makeup: "Scott said it has to start with something like Tracy singing, 'Oh, what a beautiful morning,' [from *Oklahoma*]," Shaiman recalls. "So he said, 'Good Morning, Baltimore' and pointed to the piano: 'Go play.'"

Nearly all the songs in their original score made the transition from stage to screen. Two that didn't—"Mama, I'm a Big Girl Now" and "It Takes Two"— are now heard in the background underneath spoken scenes, just one way that music can work differently on screen than on stage. Another song, Link's hard-rocking number "Ladies' Choice," was written especially for the film's needs and to suit Zac Efron's style. "We wanted something really energetic for him, to kick off that scene," says Wittman. "And we wrote it with Zac in mind." The filmmakers also capitalized on a song that had never been heard before, though it was written for the musical: "New Girl in Town." Explains Shaiman, "Adam created a montage of Tracy as she becomes a Baltimore star, and the song worked perfectly to underscore that."

It's one of the songwriters' favorites, as it gave them a chance to draw on the classic girl-group sound of the early sixties, with orchestral effects reminiscent of the famous Phil Spector "wall of sound." Throughout their careers, in fact, Shaiman and Wittman have taken on projects growing out of sixties sounds and phenomena. Their 1982 show *Livin' Dolls*, produced at the Manhattan Theater Club, was "a fastidious re-creation of the beach-party genre," as described by the *New York Times*' Frank Rich. Shaiman also worked on the 1984 revue *Leader of the Pack: The Songs of Ellie Greenwich*, featuring songs by Greenwich, Spector, and Jeff Barry, for which he had to study those records and "literally recreate them."

Original or new, virtually all the songs in the movie musical have been subtly tweaked to mesh with the screenplay and direction. "The evolution of the score is mostly a matter of stretching and refitting the existing material to the action," says Shaiman. "For example, in 'Welcome to the Sixties' on stage, there's one set change in mid-number, and a fast change of costume and look for the stars.

"On film, the song had to be kept going through a much more developed scene—from Tracy and Edna's house out into the streets and finally into Mr. Pinky's dress shop. It's now about six minutes long, constantly going back and forth between song and dialogue and visual images." The writers also added material at the end of the song. "We came up with extra licks over the ending to give John more to sing—the last sixteen bars or so is a call-and-response bit between Tracy and Edna. We wanted to take advantage of John's upper range, a range not often used when writing for our beloved Harvey Fierstein, the Broadway Edna."

Often the songwriters' work involved adding music for a dance break Adam Shankman was choreographing. "We added a whole section in the middle of 'Miss Baltimore Crabs' for the fantasy element," notes Wittman. And in the love duet between Edna and Wilbur, "Timeless to Me," Shaiman took what had been just an eight-bar dance break in the show and created new accompaniment flavored with tango rhythms and the lush orchestration of Astaire-Rodgers ballroom dance. "That was the biggest orchestra we used in the whole movie," he says.

Echoing Shankman, Shaiman says, "The songs as used in the film almost become like an opera, they are so continuous. To fit everything into the available movie time, one song may end and the next song begin moments later." As in opera, "a huge chunk of dialogue is in the songs. In a musical, when something can't be spoken, it must be sung."

Working with the movie's stellar cast of singing actors was among the team's greatest rewards. "Everything in *Hairspray* is about the characters and their emotions …and in a movie, one shot of someone's face speaks volumes," notes Wittman. "We were lucky enough to get a fabulous cast and huge stars who hit the characters so well," says Shaiman. "We didn't need to massage the songs a lot for them. No one came to us and said, 'You need to write me a new song.'"

Shaiman marvels that the deeply intentional silliness in many songs, a

Above: Marc Shaiman, Adam Shankman, Ricki Lake (the original Tracy Turnblad), and Scott Wittman in character during the finale. They play Hollywood agents who have come to watch Link perform.
Opposite left: Marc Shaiman and Scott Wittman celebrate their Tony Awards for the musical Hairspray. *Opposite right: Shaiman with John Travolta during recordings.*

tribute to the John Waters spirit, has survived intact. "We didn't need to cut anything for the actors," he says. "I just love it that John Travolta never balked at singing, 'You can't stop my happiness / 'cause I like the way I am / And you just can't stop my knife and fork / when I see a Christmas ham.' And that's how committed and confident all the performances are. The actors are really going for it."

Shaiman and Wittman joined the cast for recording sessions that took place between rehearsals and principal photography. Shaiman often had to be there in virtual form, as he was then performing on Broadway with Martin Short in the latter's *Fame Becomes Me*. Thanks to recording and Internet technologies not available even a few years ago, he could be in his New York apartment and the Toronto studio simultaneously. All the lead vocals were done during those sessions, as well as temporary backup vocals. "We wanted to put those in so the early previews could be as good as possible—we used a group of performers from the Broadway show for the temporary tracks. Later, we went back and added to them for a much more specific sound: one group like the Corny Collins white kids, another like the black kids at Maybelle's."

In contrast to that hectic period, the eight weeks Shaiman spent working on orchestrations for the film during post-production were mostly serene and solitary. Not to say restful: he was so energized by the work that he begrudged even time spent eating or showering. "I couldn't wait to get back to the keyboard and write that string line I'd been carrying around in my head for years. It's such a thrill being able to make each song sound exactly as I imagined it long ago but could never achieve with the financial and endurance constraints of a pit orchestra. Only movies give you that freedom."

There's been a potent alchemy around *Hairspray* from the start, claim the writers. As proof they offer the amazing confluence of circumstances that found them working with one of their oldest friends, Adam Shankman. "He had choreographed earlier shows I directed, and this is a project he was born to do because of his dance background," says Wittman. "The whole film looks just spectacular; it moves and flows." Shaiman remembers, on their opening night of the Broadway show, "running into Adam, who told us it was bittersweet for him: he was so happy for our success and wondering if he'd ever have a moment like this. Then we watched his career skyrocket, and he's directing this movie. It's just more of the *Hairspray* serendipity."

For these music men, witnessing the response of a new generation to *Hairspray* and its songs will be the biggest payoff of all. They have attended openings of the musical around the world, from South Africa to South Korea to Finland. They look forward eagerly to the day when the rights will be available for high schools to put it on, because finally there will be parts for the school outcasts. "The little fat girl will get to star, and the big 'fabulous' boy will get to play Edna," says Shaiman. "It will bring groups of black and white kids together by necessity."

Meanwhile, they envision this movie spreading the *Hairspray* zeitgeist in a major way. Already they've heard kids in focus groups wondering about the segregation story, "Is that how things really were back then? I can't believe that really happened." Observes Shaiman, "Tracy was ahead of her time in many ways. She's a classic musical-comedy heroine who wants to change the world and can't see why it's not possible. She drives all the action, and everyone changes around her. She has a lot in common with Dolly or Mame, except she's 16.

"The kids of the sixties are the ones who changed things, and music played a big part in it."

The full cast rehearses the finale, "You Can't Stop the Beat"; associate choreographer Jamal Simms stands in center.

From Boot Camp to Shoot

As the script was crafted and the cast puzzle assembled, other key elements of preproduction moved forward along parallel tracks. The design wizards who would help Adam Shankman create the physical world of *Hairspray* were recruited and launched into their research.

Production designer David Gropman (Academy Award–nominated for his work on *The Cider House Rules*) went location scouting, and once it became clear that Baltimore lacked the big soundstages the production would need, the filmmakers focused on Toronto, whose residential neighborhoods could be adapted to resemble John Waters's old stomping grounds. "I remember being driven up to the set of Baltimore in Toronto and feeling slightly stupefied—here was my hometown reproduced in another country," says Waters. Then Gropman embarked on his homework: first in libraries and picture collections and then on the streets of Baltimore itself.

Costume designer Rita Ryack (also an Oscar nominee, for *How the Grinch Stole Christmas*) brought major film and Broadway credits to her task of helping define the characters through dress. Time-traveling back to the era when she herself grew up, she searched for ideas, fabric, and vintage clothing in her extensive library and collection; in magazines, movies, TV shows, catalogs, and high-school yearbooks from the early sixties; and in Hollywood's research facilities, studios, and rental houses. When the time came, she gathered the crew needed on set to manage wardrobe for a big cast of actors, dancers, and extras, while building and repairing costumes on a daily basis. She and Gropman would collaborate closely on color palettes and designs, so the costumed actors always looked right on the sets they were inhabiting.

Hair designer Judi Cooper-Sealy took on a challenge of similar scope in creating styles and wigs for the multitudes who went before the camera. She had the time of her life exploring a period when hair was a big deal—literally! Makeup chief Jordan Samuel applied his expertise and experience to creating sixties looks for the actors' faces and brought in the forces to paint them for the cameras each day; while special makeup designer Tony Gardner masterminded the transformation of John Travolta's body into Edna Turnblad's by pushing the limits of prosthetics. Throughout preproduction and shooting, Adam Shankman worked closely with all the designers to merge his overall vision of the production with their concepts in each department.

On the performing side, preproduction meant revving up the rehearsal process. Although rehearsal is often kept to a bare minimum in nonmusical films, preparing to shoot a musical means getting everything right before the camera starts rolling. Shankman and his associate choreographers, having already plotted out the musical numbers in Los Angeles studio space, now were joined by some of the 130 dancers they had chosen from about 2,200 who auditioned.

Dancers had been hired specifically for how well they would meld into several groups: the Corny Collins dancers, the "Detention Kids," the dancers at Maybelle's party, and a larger group that would portray high-school kids and others at the Miss Hairspray pageant—the big finale. Even during auditions, Shankman would "segregate" the dancers to give them the sense of the divide they would embody. "For callbacks, we would separate the Detention Kids from the Council kids. I would make the black kids sit on one side of the room and the white kids on the other side, and ask them, 'How does this feel?' They got the feeling very quickly."

While still in Los Angeles, Shankman and his choreographers began working with the younger stars, who had lots of difficult dancing to get in their bodies: Efron, Bynes, Snow, and Kelley, as well as Nikki Blonksy. Vocal

Above, left to right: Anne Fletcher; Taylor Parks (Little Inez) with associate choreographer Joey Pizzi, and a trio of dancers.

training, too, began months before the shoot, with the most of the principals working privately on their technique. They also started learning their songs very early. *Hairspray*'s music supervisor, Matt Sullivan, (who fulfilled the same function on *Chicago, Dreamgirls*, and *Rent*) oversaw all aspects of the music production. Christopher Walken was grateful for the early one-on-one coaching he received. "They showed me the routine and gave me the song on tape. I took that home and walked around the house, listening to it, just absorbing it. The best way to learn these things is slowly, just take your time."

Then, when the rehearsal operation moved to Toronto, "the factory started in earnest," says Shankman. First with the Corny Collins Council dancers learning their routines. Then the Detention kids arrived and went to work in another room, soon to be joined by the women playing the Dynamites girl group.

Once the principal actors arrived on the scene, "it was like a three-ring circus," recalls Craig Zadan. Different rehearsal rooms were earmarked for song rehearsals, vocal coaching, dance training, acting and scene work, and every day a given actor would shuttle in and out of various rooms. They'd practice and refine songs endlessly, because, as Sullivan says, "You want the actor to know the song inside and out, the melody, the timing—so that eventually they can concentrate on the acting and getting the character through the song." In the dance room, the associate choreographers would be working with dance ensembles or principals, getting the numbers into their bones. In yet another room, actors would be rehearsing spoken scenes. "It was a scheduling nightmare," says Shankman, "but it was so cool for me—I got to run from room to room and make little changes and fix things; talk to the actors about choices they were making."

It was exhausting for the actors, but they had fun with it too. "It was like

Above: From left: New Line co-chairman Michael Lynne, executive producers Jennifer Gibgot and Garrett Grant, Adam Shankman, Craig Zadan, Neil Meron, and associate choreographer Joey Pizzi.

school," says Travolta. "You woke up every morning and went to one period after another: music rehearsal, dance rehearsal, scene rehearsal. Wardrobe fittings and musical tests. Dancing tests. Musical-number-with-costume tests. All day long, just like in an old MGM production. And that's the magic of a musical—it's too bad we don't get to do them very often."

The two-month-long process in Toronto led up to two major events. On a movie musical, the time between rehearsals and shooting film is when the music is actually recorded. Vocals and instrumental backgrounds are prerecorded in these sessions; later, when film is rolling, the performers sing to the tracks. Those unfamiliar with the practice might wonder why this critical stage is squeezed into this time slot. Craig Zadan explains: "When you start the rehearsal period, an actor doesn't know the character he's playing. If you start recording vocals too soon, the actors don't really know how to perform the number, and you haven't had the benefit of setting tempos. So you actually record the vocals as late as possible."

But still before the filming takes place. Matt Sullivan notes that "we prerecord the music to have control over the quality. Where you're on the set, it's noisy, you have people dancing, shuffling feet. When you have a prerecorded track, it's nice and clean." Sullivan was impressed by the level of preparation everyone brought to the recording sessions. "Everyone walked into each session fully ready to go."

The true climax of rehearsals, though, was the crucial "table read," when the entire cast gathers to read—and sing—through the entire show for the first time. It's the only time during the production when all the principal actors are together in the same place for a few hours, because of the vagaries of shooting and personal schedules. "So Michelle Pfeiffer gets to see Queen Latifah's scenes and songs, and vice versa," notes Craig Zadan. "Everybody gets

Above James Marsden and dancers. Right: A long day of rehearsing. Below: Elijah Kelley and Taylor Parks with Detention Kids.

to see each person do their thing, and they understand how they fit into the whole movie."

For Adam Shankman, it was a day full of anxiety and thrills. "It was the first time I'd sat down with all the actors for the first time. To be in a room with that much talent, and watch everybody riffing off each other—and I'm sitting across the table from Michelle Pfeiffer and John Travolta and Christopher Walken … hey, I'm not above getting star-struck. Even though there was a lot of work still to be done, it was so incredible to watch people break down and cry when someone sang their song. And when the dancers would get up and perform a number, I saw so much inspiration wash onto them. I remember thinking this was a moment that will change my life forever, and change me inside."

The filmmakers already knew what they'd found in Nikki Blonsky, but the table read sealed it. Recalls Neil Meron, "She humbled the great stars that we had in this movie. They sat there with their jaws to the ground watching her. It was one of those great experiences where you just can't believe your eyes."

Also attending, to observe and help as needed with the songs, were composer Marc Shaiman and his colyricist, Scott Wittman. For them, it was the day when this new *Hairspray* took on the magic they knew so well from their stage musical. "Even the stars were star-struck," remembers Shaiman. "Michelle Pfeiffer, for instance, didn't know the material that well, but at the reading you saw her take in the whole show. And you could see emotion coming over her face—especially toward the end when Maybelle sings 'I Know Where I've Been.' That song is sort of the point of the whole story. So for these movie stars, who maybe have taken a role for various reasons of their own—on that day you could feel them come together, wanting to be part of this, for all the best reasons."

Finally, the *Hairspray* cast and crew launched into a 13-week shoot in which

all their hard work was captured on celluloid. They were more than ready. Says Queen Latifah: "You've been rehearsing so much that you can't wait to put it on screen." Quite a few sequences were filmed in outdoor locations around Toronto, and as autumn went on, cast and crew donned warm outerwear—except John Travolta in his heavy makeup, who always welcomed a cool breeze.

Cinematographer Bojan Bazelli (*Mr. and Mrs. Smith*) and his camera crew captured the big production numbers with batteries of cameras that provided views from many angles—far from the standard tactics of shooting a musical as if it were onstage. "Our goal was to capture the body language of the dancers, and all the emotion the dancing conveys," he says. "I think these are some of the best dance numbers ever filmed."

Teams from wardrobe, hair, makeup, and set decoration engaged in furious activity to get scenes and talent ready for action at the appointed times. A typical day for John Travolta would begin with four hours of heavy prosthetic work. Actors and dancers would gather en masse to film the big musical numbers, which might take several days, or the whole effort could be squeezed into one long, intense day. Zac Efron notes with amazement that "The Nicest Kids in Town," which he'd been practicing every day for two months, "was shot in a single day—ten hours of filming."

During a break, Jerry Stiller reminisced about doing the original movie with John Waters in 1988 and marveled at the contrasts. "On that set, we had the kind of freedom that comes with desperation. If you didn't have enough film, you left the shot in the camera. If a boom happened to get in the frame, it stayed there. At the wrap party, I think we had cream cheese and jelly sandwiches, which is a far cry from the lovely catering here. But we were all so caught up in it and having so much fun—and really being freed ourselves, in our performances. I never wanted to leave Baltimore."

> *"You want the actor to know the song inside and out, the melody, the timing—so that eventually they can concentrate on the acting and getting the character through the song."*
> — *Music supervisor Matt Sullivan*

For Adam Shankman these weeks were an exhausting but glorious blur of nonstop activity. He was still choreographing and rescripting the big finale, "Can't Stop the Beat," well into shooting. Department heads got used to him showing up at any given moment to check on a costume, a wig, or a street sign. And he still had several months of editing and other postproduction work looming ahead. It didn't matter.

"Emotionally this film changed me because I achieved something I'd always hoped for," he says. "And with a group of people who trusted me in a way I never thought possible, because of the stylized nature of the material. For these high-octane actors to express that kind of trust—it's such a leap of faith. I think that helped me grow as a director and let me do things I haven't done in the past."

Soundtrack to Life

Hairspray wrapped on December 8, 2006, and the filmmakers, cast, and crew went their separate ways—not without some final thoughts on what they had done together, how audiences might respond, and this film's place in the *Hairspray* galaxy and the universe of movie musicals.

Making *Hairspray* for 2007 was a balancing act: to bring its style into the present through realistic characterizations and kinetic photography, yet hold tight to the sixties zeitgeist at the story's core. The early sixties, that is, when America was teetering on the edge of something truly new, an energy for change that was just starting to detonate. Emblematic of this was the way pop music danced into our consciousness and took root as never before. It became the soundtrack to our lives, as we hear in this movie's constant musical underlay. The songs take over. "We shot 'You Can't Stop The Beat' over nine days," recalls Neil Meron, "and never got tired of it. You went home with it in your head. You woke up with it in the morning, you had lunch with it. The whole score becomes part of the fabric of your life—and what great songs to have there!"

In the sixties, music brought people together, in Baltimore and across the country. Musicals are the most communal form of movies, for the same reasons. The tunes and the beat move us, bond us, make us want to join in.

And we recognize real talent when we see it; we admire people who can sing and dance wonderfully. It's no accident, thinks actor James Marsden, that the most popular reality shows are ones like *American Idol* and *Dancing with the Stars.* "Those are the only reality shows I can watch because you're seeing somebody with talent do something amazing." *Hairspray* is part of a surging wave of new movie musicals that are drawing audiences in the same way.

Tracy's story takes place in 1962, a time both like and unlike the present. We perceive it as a much more innocent time, and in that way *Hairspray* gives people a break from the chaos, cynicism and complexity of 2007. "While directing the Broadway production, Jack O'Brien would remind his cast that they needed to hang onto and project that innocence, even when delivering some of the risqué lyrics or dialogue," says Marc Shaiman.

Hairspray's young stars see the sixties as history, their parents' time. They're amazed at how very different things were then, from manners to dress to technology. Zac Efron marvels at what kids managed to do without: "Cell phones; today there's kids in preschool who have them. No bottled water, no HDTV or X-Box, no seatbelts or airbags." He knows of the sixties from his mom, who watched *American Bandstand* as a teen. "And when I was growing up, every time that music would come on, she would jump into the Twist, or one of those dances. Never in a million years did I think I'd ever do the Twist in a scene. I can't tell you how much that made me laugh inside. I'm playing, maybe, the kind of guy my mom probably had a crush on."

But some things haven't changed much. The focus in *Hairspray* is on outsiders, the kind of people John Waters always put at the center of his movies. The Turnblad family, Tracy and her friend Penny, the kids they befriend—they all are different, rejected by the in-crowd. "To me, a fat girl basically stands for every outsider," says Waters. And the pressure to conform socially today isn't any less than in 1962, certainly for teens. "The themes still ring true, which is

why I think *Hairspray*'s been a success in every incarnation," says Neil Meron.

"For one thing, the idea of the underdog being able to step out in front and effect change is completely relevant. We're also dealing with issues like body image, which is in every newspaper and magazine. This is about loving the way God made you, being comfortable in your body and saying, 'You're going to accept me no matter what I look like, because here I am and I can make a contribution.'"

Queen Latifah sees the movie's themes through her character's eyes. "We're dealing with what is considered 'beautiful' and what should be put out there in front of the cameras for the world to see. We're dealing with people who have real talent versus people who don't, but maybe they have the right look. We're dealing with people who need to come out of their shell and live, like Edna Turnblad." Edna, you could say, embodies 1950s America stuck in its safe, confined world, but about to bust out into the sixties.

And though we've come far on civil rights, no one believes that American society has freed itself from racial bias. For young audiences, dramatizing that black and white kids couldn't even dance together on TV 40 years ago will be a history lesson more powerful than textbooks can convey. Growing up in Georgia, Elijah Kelley absorbed civil rights history firsthand "from people that actually marched. Even when I was growing up, people were told, you can't date that race, you can't do this. Why? That's what I think about and that's what drives me. That's the underlying statement in the movie.

"It's 40 years ago, but you've got to think that some parents are still passing on those attitudes to their children. So we have to keep talking about

it. And it's the music where everybody comes together. In the finale, you can see it on people's faces—the spirit of it, the energy of it. You can see the harmony and the camaraderie between the races. Music transcends color, everything. It makes you move, makes you happy, makes you sad; it makes you remember things."

Just as in 1962, we're always looking for heroes to help us find the way. "Tracy is just the hope of the future for me," says Shankman. "Like all of us, she finds it really easy to want things for herself. And then, unlike many of us, she comes to realize there's more to the world than what one person wants. It's about community, and helping the greater good.

"At the end of the day, what I hope people will leave the movie theater with—besides feeling great and dancing in the aisles—is that this movie is all about the underdog."

Adds Neil Meron, "It sends you out of the movie theater wanting to dance and to think. And that's a fine accomplishment."

Right: Nikki Blonsky and Ricki Lake, the current and former Tracy Turnblad.

part two

The Story on Screen and Behind the Scenes

"It's changing out there, Ma. You'll like it. People who are different ... their time is coming."

— *Tracy Turnblad*

Over the signature drum riff of a girl-group song, we see a wide shot of Baltimore, circa 1962. The camera moves in on a working-class neighborhood, and still closer, on a nondescript corner storefront ... the Hardy Har Hut joke shop. In the apartment upstairs, a teenage girl is waking up ... as always, with a hopeful smile on her face and an insistent dance beat in her head. Tracy Turnblad, a girl with big hair, big dreams and an even bigger heart, dances through her home and out into the street on her way to school: *"Good Morning, Baltimore!"* The bus leaves without her, but no problem ... she hitches a ride on a garbage truck, still singing her heart out. Wherever Tracy is, the music goes with her.

"Good Morning, Baltimore!"

Woke up today
Feeling the way I always do ...
Hungry for something
that I can't eat
Then I hear the beat ...

That rhythm of town
starts calling me down ...

And some day
when I take to the floor
the world's gonna wake up and see
Baltimore and me!

Look at my hair!

Nikki Blonsky
as Tracy Turnblad

"I always wanted to play Tracy Turnblad. I always wanted to be in Hairspray," says 17-year-old Nikki Blonsky. And in a dream-come-true tale that's already become Hollywood legend, that's just what happened. Nikki, who had performed in school musicals and operas but never professionally, was scooping ice cream at Long Island's Coldstone Creamery when she was invited to try out for her dream role. She braved a blizzard in Manhattan to meet Hairspray's casting directors, and, after weeks of intense scrutiny by the filmmakers, came away with the prize.

"We had to find a real teenager who could not only sing, dance, act and project strength and total vulnerability as well as indomitable warmth, but was also *fat*, not chubby, and pretty," says Shankman. "And then Nikki waltzed in. It was magic." He was determined to cast an unknown, and Ricki Lake, who was likewise plucked from nowhere to be the original Tracy in 1988, explains: "I think it's really important for the audience to fall in love with Tracy and not know her from anywhere else."

When cast and filmmakers gathered for the first table read, Nikki's powerful singing and stage presence blew everyone away—including her famous costars. John Travolta compared her to the young Streisand. Says Adam Shankman, "Nikki has really surpassed my expectations and dreams. She learned so quickly, it's scary. She's out there dancing like a maniac with intensely talented professional dancers. Doing scene work with John Travolta, Michelle Pfeiffer, Chris Walken ... and she's making them up their game because she is the character. She's a really special talent and a really special girl."

Nikki had the time of her life during the rigorous rehearsal and shooting process, while working harder than she ever imagined. She marvels that her director and coaches sought her creative input—"They would say, does this feel like something Tracy would do?"—and was happy to discover that her colleagues were "not just an amazing actor or producer or director or choreographer, they're real, wonderful human beings. I feel so fortunate to have spent this time with them working on such an incredible project." She's also thrilled with the messages Tracy and Hairspray bring to audiences: that heart means way more than looks, that the fight against prejudice of every kind has to be carried on by each new generation. "I can't tell you how proud I was to be holding that sign, 'Integration Not Segregation' ... to be playing Tracy, who believes in the same things I do. This movie is coming out to help push those issues forward again."

Baltimore, Ontario

On the *Hairspray* map, the city of Baltimore has always been more than mere geography. In John Waters's movie, his gritty hometown was like another character in the story, a strong personality all its own. Songwriters Shaiman and Wittman recognized this and made their show's opening number "Good Morning, Baltimore!" But shooting the movie musical on location in Baltimore was ruled out for lack of infrastructure. Waters jokes, "The day they announced it wasn't going to be shot in Baltimore, I ran out of town."

Could another location fill in convincingly for Baltimore? Production designer David Gropman had the task of making sure. Gropman had a deep background in both theater and film design, having worked with Robert Altman on the Broadway stage version of *Come Back to the Five and Dime, Jimmy Dean, Jimmy Dean*, then a number of that great director's films, as well as projects with Lasse Hällstrom, Robert Benton, and Steve Zaillian.

"For me the most important thing is to know where the story takes place," says Gropman. "And if we're not going to shoot in the actual place, then it's critical to have all the information you could possibly need about Baltimore in 1962 in your back pocket. So that every location you choose, every set you design, every detail you call out is informed by that background."

Gropman's work began on several parallel fronts: delving into the script,

meeting with the director, investigating Baltimore, and "a trip to the library to start researching Baltimore in 1962." From the script he learned that the story would take place on some 30 locations. "So you're researching the skyline and storefronts and residential streets. You're also looking at the interiors of all kinds of shops, as well as schools and residences." Picture research was essential because, as producer Neil Meron points out, "Lots of stuff that existed in 1962 in Baltimore is no longer there." Movie magic would have to make up for the losses.

Gropman also went to Baltimore to get a feel for the real thing. "For three days I toured the city with the film commissioner, seeing the Highland Town neighborhood where the Waters film was shot, and other neighborhoods." He noted distinctive details of how buildings were constructed and ornamented— in particular the "form stone" used on homes in those working-class areas. "It was a fake stone veneer applied to houses, to spruce them up. Form stone is such a signature of Baltimore from that period, I knew we had to use it." On later trips, his team took impressions from real facades and created molds in their shop. They made form stone for the Turnblad house, other homes on Tracy's block, and some commercial exteriors.

The second key factor, says Gropman, is being in sync with your director,

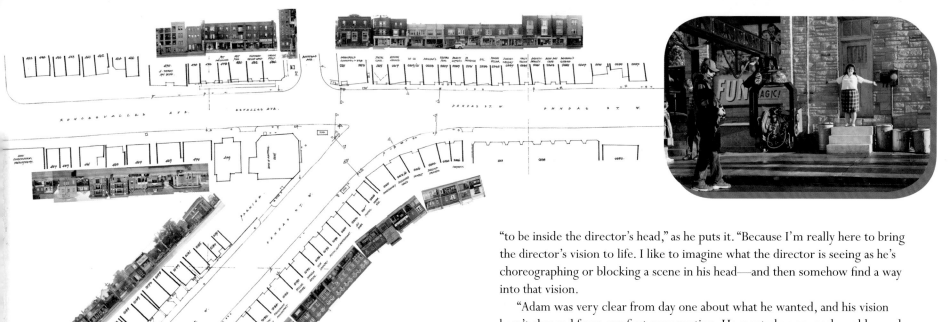

Above: Production design diagram of the intersection. Top right: Shooting Tracy outside the Turnblad house. Below: Composite of the Baltimore commercial intersection created in Toronto. Period vehicles wait at the curb for use in a shot.

"to be inside the director's head," as he puts it. "Because I'm really here to bring the director's vision to life. I like to imagine what the director is seeing as he's choreographing or blocking a scene in his head—and then somehow find a way into that vision.

"Adam was very clear from day one about what he wanted, and his vision hasn't changed from our first conversation. He wanted a very real world, a real Baltimore. He didn't want the look to be theatrical or exaggerated. At first you're sort of testing the waters, making sure: does he really mean that? But every time we'd have a question or look at a color, look at a piece of detail, that's exactly what he wanted. Even so, it wasn't until we stepped onto our first set that I was absolutely convinced. From then on, I always felt sure about which way to go. Sometimes he might be a little surprised by a detail or a color, and enjoy the surprise. But mostly my aim is that when he walks onto a set, he feels totally at home."

Next, Gropman went to Toronto—a major filmmaking capital these days— to evaluate it as a stand-in for Baltimore. "I needed to determine how well the film's exterior locations could be served by Toronto," says Gropman. "And by the time Adam arrived a few days later, I felt fine about it. Toronto is in no way an identical match to Baltimore. But there were resemblances: in the use of form stone, the awnings, the street signs. Enough to make me feel it could work.

"But more importantly there is a spirit to the architecture there, and a scale to certain neighborhoods that just felt right for the movie." Another advantage, adds Neil Meron, was "finding neighborhoods in Toronto that were virtually unchanged from the early sixties."

Research continued once Gropman's crew set up in Toronto. "The art department coordinator and our intern were constantly pulling more information," he says. Gropman found the rhythms of filming a musical congenial to his design process: the long rehearsal period allowed him to collaborate closely with Shankman, and because the choreography was worked out in preproduction, he was provided up front with information about what sets should look like and how they had to function. "Often Adam would have conceived and choreographed a piece before I even sat down to start a design or make a ground plan. I would see a number and already know how the space had to work."

A huge test of Gropman's designs, his crew's capacities, and Toronto's

raw material came up early in the shoot. By just the fourth day of filming, they needed to shoot two big numbers on the production's biggest set—a commercial intersection where both "Good Morning, Baltimore!" and "Welcome to the Sixties" take place. "It was the real test of whether we had created 1962 Baltimore, involving an enormous amount of effort and lumber and paint," says Gropman. "There were 60-odd exterior façades to deal with, a few residential but most commercial. Almost all required signage, reworking of windows and storefronts. Adding awnings on the second or third floors. We reproduced a certain kind of aluminum awning from the period; you see them all over Baltimore even now.

"If you had asked me beforehand, I probably would have said it was impossible. But we had a wonderful team of people who made it happen."

On top of everything, he adds, "'Good Morning, Baltimore!' is the scene where John Waters appears in a cameo. I was thrilled to have a chance to meet him, and of course a bit nervous about how he would react to the set. But before I could even introduce myself, he came over and said, 'Wow, this looks just like Baltimore. This is exactly what you would see in 1962.' So, phew."

Waters confirms: "It really looked like Highland Town. It's amazing, but that's what movie magic can do. I saw everybody walking around wearing Baltimore T-shirts, carrying the *Baltimore Sun*, and thought, I'm in another country."

Gropman drops a hint that the new film will contain some visual homage to Waters's 1988 film. "I'm not going to say where, but I've tried for a couple of winks to the original *Hairspray*. It's a beautifully designed film and I wanted to pay tribute."

Opposite: Director Adam Shankman and views of Tracy on her way to school. Above: From left to right, production designer David Gropman, art director Dennis Davenport, art department coordinator Dusty Reeves, and first assistant art directors Aleks Marinkovich and David Fremlin at the studio complex in Toronto. Below: Commercial street with signage created by the art department.

Music in the Air

With musicals, on screen the big question is: how do you make it seem right and natural that people are singing? Adam Shankman wanted to get that out of the way at the beginning. "With 'Good Morning, Baltimore' I was asked, do you want to have the chorus, the people on the streets, lip-sync the background vocals? I struggled with that, thinking, if they didn't sing, then where would all those voices be coming from?" Yet he didn't really want the passersby to sing—it felt too theatrical—so he invented a plausible source for the singing: "My idea was that the first time you hear an outside choral voice, it's coming from the TV. Tracy turns on the TV, and it's playing a show called 'Good Morning, Baltimore.' Our song is the theme song.

"Once you've heard the voices, hopefully you just buy that they keep going, only in her head. She walks down the street, and no one pays any attention to her while she's singing, other than the people she acknowledges. And you understand that she's this incredibly happy, cheery girl who hears life as a song. It's like her imaginary world. And the very next song is the theme song to *The Corny Collins Show*, which comes from the TV, too. Now there are two numbers with that kind of justification. From then on, I think, the audience goes with you because the musical form has been set."

"If we're not going to shoot in the actual place, then it's critical to have all the information you could possibly need about Baltimore in 1962 in your back pocket. So that every location you choose, every set you design, every detail you call out is informed by that background."
—David Gropman

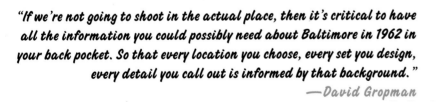

At school the hours crawl by like a 45 record played at 33 rpm. In Miss Wimsey's classroom, a geeky kid gets Tracy in trouble because he can't see over her teased-up hair. But beneath that amazing 'do, the beat goes on through class after boring class, until she's sprung by the afternoon bell. With her best girlpal Penny Pingleton, Tracy races home to catch the daily broadcast of The Corny Collins Show, a Baltimore TV dance program "brought to you by Ultra-Clutch Hairspray ... for hair that holds up even in a NASA wind tunnel!" The show's main attraction is a team of young dancers known as the Corny Collins Council — all good-looking, squeaky clean, and strictly Caucasian. As Corny introduces them in "The Nicest Kids in Town," they sound off roll-call like Mouseketeers ... "Brad ... Tammy ... Brenda ... Fender ... Lou Ann ... Joey ... Noreen ...!" Then there's Link Larkin, a dark-haired heartthrob who makes Tracy and Penny scream. And, of course, Amber Von Tussle, a perky b[...] with a heart of ice, who makes nice for the camera but elbows [...] stage at every chance.

12 WYZT TELEVISION

James Marsden as Corny Collins

When James Marsden was up for the part of Corny Collins, he had famous friends rooting for him. "Both Hugh Jackman, his co-star in *X-Men*, and his director, Bryan Singer, told us, 'You've got to hire Jimmy,'" recalls producer Craig Zadan. But he needed no help beyond his own versatility and clean-scrubbed, all-American looks. "I kept saying, I want a young Dick Clark, and he shouldn't be that much older than the kids," says Adam Shankman.

Like most people in Hollywood, the director associated Marsden with his action roles in *X-Men* and *Superman Returns*. But a few knew that he also had a killer singing voice, which he showcased on an episode of *Ally McBeal*. Casting director David Rubin showed Shankman a tape of that performance, "and the casting process stopped there. I went: That's my guy."

Marsden had been looking for a chance to use his musical talent, and this dual-identity role let him exercise his considerable acting chops as well. In his public persona of dance show host Corny Collins, "he's a mix of Dick Clark and Ryan Seacrest, with a few dollops of cheese on top," says the actor. "I mean, his name's Corny—it's like a free pass to be over the top and smooth and ... corny." But off camera, the character has to hold his own with Michelle Pfeiffer's Velma, as he pushes to integrate the show's dancers. "He's excited about black music becoming a powerful force, and

he welcomes that," Marsden notes. "At the end of the day, you have to believe that these people are not just caricatures. I think the creators have done a wonderful job in getting to the emotional core of the story under the glossy veneer."

Singing was always a hobby for Marsden, aside from a few professional appearances. A fan of the great vocal stylists, from Sinatra to Dean Martin to Bobby Darin, he was "familiar with their styles and what they did with their voices. When I heard Corny's songs, it was obvious to me what I needed to do. I immediately pictured Bobby Darin snapping his fingers and winking at the camera. I just stole all their little moves." His cast-mates noticed, says Zac Efron. "There's isn't a moment when he's not trying to figure out how to do something cooler, make something look better, use different inflections. He's constantly working."

Marsden is excited to be part of what he sees as a major revival of movie musicals— especially in one that has something to say while showing people a great time. "I think some films have gotten a little too dark and nihilistic, and it's nice to come back to something that's mostly fun and kind," he says. "When we can get to a point where we can embrace each other, embrace our individuality and realize that's what makes us special, then we'll be in a better place.

"It's been like a gift," he declares. "You can feel on the set that everybody's here because they want to be. They love the music and their characters. And they want to give audiences something to cheer for."

Corny
Hey there, Teenage Baltimore! Don't change that channel! It's time for the Corny Collins Show!

"I think that what Adam and Craig and Neil and everybody on board this movie is doing is to take the colorful, wonderful, genius music from the Broadway show, and the great characters from John Waters's movie, and breathing new life into them."
— James Marsden

"The Nicest Kids in Town"
You better come on down
and meet the Nicest Kids in Town —
nice white kids
who like to lead the way
And once a month
we have our "Negro Day"

And I'm the man who keeps it
spinning round
Mr. Corny Collins
with the latest, greatest

"There's so much emotion going into the singing and dancing. All the dancers who play the Corny Council are amazing—I've been really lucky to spend so much time with them. They're all so talented and really cute, with huge dance moves and smiles all the time. The moment Adam yells 'Action!' they go crazy."
— *Brittany Snow*

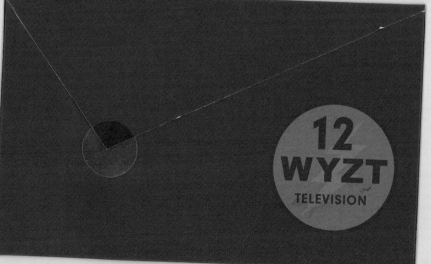

12 **WYZT** TELEVISION

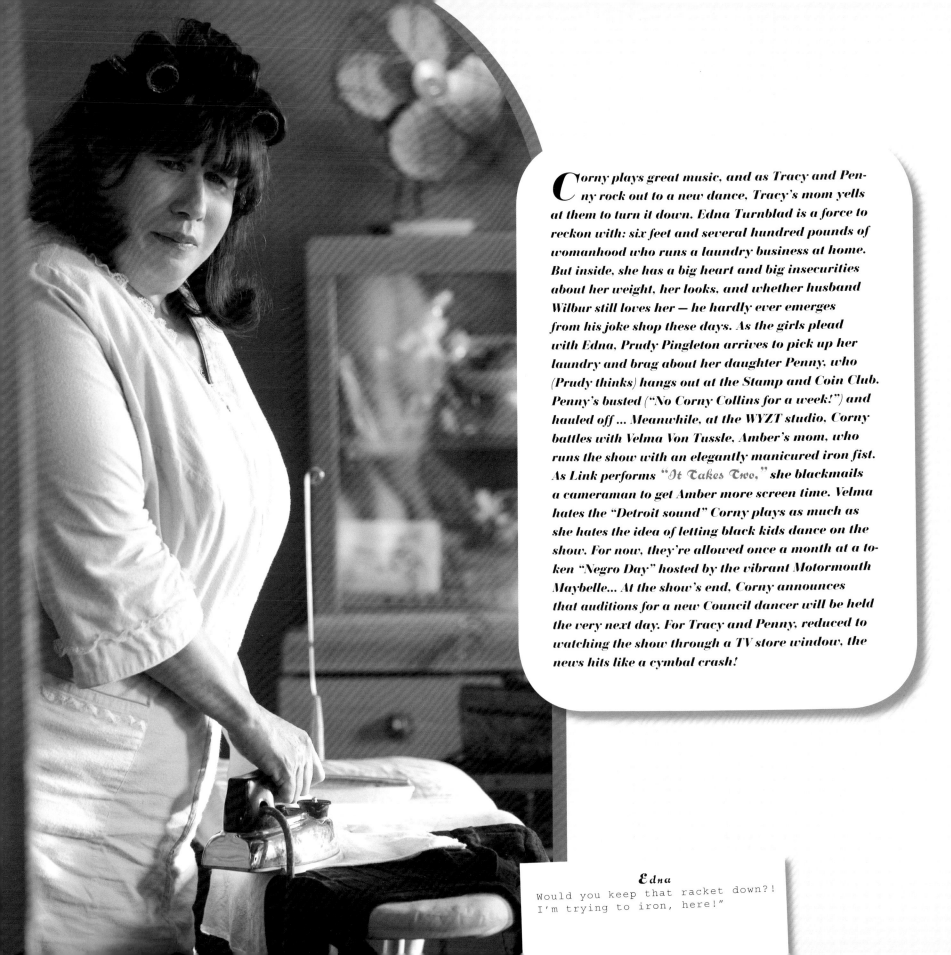

*C*orny plays great music, and as Tracy and Penny rock out to a new dance, Tracy's mom yells at them to turn it down. Edna Turnblad is a force to reckon with: six feet and several hundred pounds of womanhood who runs a laundry business at home. But inside, she has a big heart and big insecurities about her weight, her looks, and whether husband Wilbur still loves her — he hardly ever emerges from his joke shop these days. As the girls plead with Edna, Prudy Pingleton arrives to pick up her laundry and brag about her daughter Penny, who (Prudy thinks) hangs out at the Stamp and Coin Club. Penny's busted ("No Corny Collins for a week!") and hauled off ... Meanwhile, at the WYZT studio, Corny battles with Velma Von Tussle, Amber's mom, who runs the show with an elegantly manicured iron fist. As Link performs *"It Takes Two,"* she blackmails a cameraman to get Amber more screen time. Velma hates the "Detroit sound" Corny plays as much as she hates the idea of letting black kids dance on the show. For now, they're allowed once a month at a token "Negro Day" hosted by the vibrant Motormouth Maybelle... At the show's end, Corny announces that auditions for a new Council dancer will be held the very next day. For Tracy and Penny, reduced to watching the show through a TV store window, the news hits like a cymbal crash!

Edna
Would you keep that racket down?!
I'm trying to iron, here!"

At Home with the Turnblads

Tracy and her parents live in a typical Baltimore row house, circa mid-20th-century, in a lower-middle-class neighborhood much like Highland Town, where John Waters once lived. Built most likely in the 1920s or '30s of brick or wood siding, such homes often had form-stone detailing, a first-floor bay window, and small backyards verging on an alleyway. The production found a street in residential Toronto that was close enough to the real thing for exterior shots but created the interior rooms on a soundstage.

These neighborhoods often mixed in commercial enterprises—as at the Turnblads, where the first floor is occupied by Wilbur's business. The distinctive signage for the Hardy Har Hut sets the house apart: it's no ordinary family that lives here. An exterior detail borrowed from Baltimore was a painted screen door in front. "That was another signature for Baltimore in that period and even earlier," says David Gropman. "Painted window screens and front-door screens with scenic renditions of cottages in the woods, or rolling hills, meandering paths. I guess they brought a sense of the rural into these urban neighborhoods."

Upstairs, the set decorators made sure that everything in the apartment was true to the late 1950s/early 1960s, from furnishings to kitchen appliances to the rabbit-eared TV broadcasting *The Corny Collins Show* … right down to Edna's iron. The Hardy Har Hut had its own amazing interior, but Gropman tried to mingle the decor of home and shop to show the same personality at work in both. "I pulled elements and colors used in the Turnblad apartment upstairs down to the store interior. We used a lot of varnished wood and my

beloved green—we brought that into the Hardy Har space as well. We tried to make the apartment a mostly monochromatic world, so that when Edna finally steps out of it, she confronts a big change in colors and textures."

Director of photography Bojan Bazelli and his camera crew took great pains to avoid the look of interiors that are obviously created on a soundstage, especially in the Turnblad apartment set. A giveaway is often that that the set is lighted from above, because it's easier that way. "Normally ceilings are removable for shooting, but here we worked with production design to build a box with a fixed seven-foot ceiling, which forced us to be more original and creative in lighting," says Bazelli. "The camera angles often include the ceiling, so it looks like a real location, with light coming only from the windows —or at night from 'practical' lights such as table lamps" (but with stronger bulbs). "It gave a more intimate look than typical studio photography, a sense of real space."

The set makes it clear that the Turnblads inhabit a working-class environment, which sets the tone for how Tracy is treated when she auditions for *The Corny Collins Show*. "Being told she's not good enough and doesn't look right," says Gropman. "She doesn't have enough sweater sets in her closet. These people have what they need and not much more. But they have a lot of love in that house."

"The Turnblads definitely live in a working-class neighborhood. These people have what they need and not much more. But they have a lot of love in that house."

—Production designer David Gropman

Opposite: The exterior of the Turnblad house showing the joke shop entrance, and (top), the apartment interior created on a soundstage. This page, above: details of the interior, including elements that "migrated" upstairs from the joke shop. Right: Dancers on the Buddy Deane Show.

Dancing on TV

We love watching people dance on TV. Almost since the boob tube first invaded American homes—roughly coinciding with the rise of rock 'n' roll—we've gathered around our sets to watch dancers rock out to records or guest artists lip-synching their hits. The plot of *Hairspray* tracks a phenomenon that stretches from *The Arthur Murray Party* through *Soul Train* to *Dancing with the Stars*.

The paradigm for *The Corny Collins Show* was *American Bandstand*, the proto-dance party show that arose in Philadelphia in 1952, went national with peppy host Dick Clark, and stayed on the air until 1989. *Bandstand* created the familiar format of kids dancing to hit records, with a core of "Philly Regulars" who became idols to young fans. In its heyday, the show aired every day, anchoring many a high schooler's afternoon. Clark, of course, became a household name and the show spawned scores of imitators.

John Waters's Baltimore model was *The Buddy Deane Show*, which aired on WJZ-TV from 1957 to 1964. Its host was Winston "Buddy" Deane, a former radio DJ from Little Rock and one of the first in Baltimore to regularly play rock 'n' roll. (Deane had a cameo in the Waters film as a TV reporter.) For a time, *Buddy Deane* was the most popular local show in the nation, airing for 2-1/2 hours a day, six days a week, before being taken off the air because it refused to integrate black and white dancers.

Like *Bandstand*, the Deane show was built around a stable of regular dancers known as "the Committee." As Waters recalls, they were initially recruited from local teen centers to dance with the guests. "To be selected, you had to bring a 'character reference' letter, qualify in a dance audition, and show in an interview that you had 'personality.'" At first dancers cycled off the Committee every few months, but soon it turned into a popularity contest with viewers sending fan mail to their favorites, "so a star system was born."

To Waters (a one-time guest on the program) and his cohorts, the show ruled their social life. "If you couldn't do the Buddy Deane Jitterbug, you were a social outcast," he says. "And because a new dance was introduced practically every week, you had to watch every day to keep up. It was maddening…."

New York City kids watched The Clay Cole Show from 1959 to 1964. And the list goes on: *Hullaballoo* and *Shindig* were prime-time musical variety shows of the sixties that featured dancers. The influential *Soul Train* in the sixties showcased R&B, soul, and later hip-hop acts. The MTV era brought a slew of other shows including *Club MTV, Dance Fever, Strictly Dancing*, and *Dance Party USA* (where future talk show host Kelly Ripa was a regular dancer). Today, *Dancing with the Stars* combines classic elements of the TV dance shows with celebrity mania, cutthroat competition, and Internet voting. Then there's *Bandwagon*, a program out of Mankato, Minnesota, featuring polkas and other ultra-square fare, with a studio audience dancing along. Now in its 46th year, it may be the longest-running TV dance party ever.

In the Turnblad living room, Tracy begs for permission to do the audition, but Edna is adamantly against it. Tracy's upbeat ambitions feel like a reproach to Edna's own confined existence. Besides, she really loves her big little girl and worries that if Tracy gives people an opening, they'll pick on her because of her size. The argument turns to hair ... Tracy defends her style by pointing to Jackie Kennedy's bouffant, while clueless Edna claims that the First Lady's hair is "naturally stiff." After Tracy storms off to her room, Wilbur goes to console her ... and ends up taking her side. "This is America, babe! You gotta think big to be big!"

Edna
No one in this house is
auditioning for anything!

Edna
For your information, missy, I once dreamed I'd own a coin-operated laundromat!

Tracy
Dancing on that show is my dream!

Wilbur
Then you go for it! This is America, babe! You gotta think big to be big!

Given that Edna would be played by a male actor, and that *Hairspray* needed star power to match its scope, casting John Travolta was a no-brainer. As producer Neil Meron notes, "When you do a movie musical, you want to ground it in a musical sensibility. John Travolta, we think, says movie musical, in the great tradition of Fred Astaire and Gene Kelly—for this generation. No other actor could bring the musical gifts he brings to the character of Edna, who is now such a rich, three-dimensional rich character who can sing and dance. And break your heart."

Travolta burst onto the big screen back in the 1970s, as Danny Zucko in *Grease* and Tony Manero in *Saturday Night Fever*. His musical gifts may have seemed innate, but came from a combination of genes and hard work. "My family is from musical comedies," he explains. "My sister was in the first Broadway production of *Gypsy* with Ethel Merman in 1961. Then she did that whole generation of musicals, *Irma La Douce* and *Bye Bye Birdie* and *Carnival*. My mother was more of a dramatic actress; her orientation was straight plays."

Travolta's mom enrolled him in drama school as a teen. He took to it like a duck to water, and left school at 16 to pursue his own musical theater career. "For maybe 12 years, I performed on Broadway, off Broadway, summer theatre, touring companies—you name it." At 18, he got his first Broadway role in the New York production of *Grease*, followed by the Andrews Sisters musical *Over Here*. But Hollywood beckoned.

In film, though, Travolta's career largely coincided with the period when musicals were Hollywood poison. So after the nostalgia hit *Grease* and the dancing-but-no-singing triumph of *Saturday Night Fever*, Travolta went on to become famous for everything but musical comedy: his dramatic roles in films like *Urban Cowboy*, *A Civil Action*, *Primary Colors*, and *Pulp Fiction*, and classic comedy parts like Chili Palmer in *Get Shorty*. He turned down Billy Flynn in *Chicago* (to his admitted regret later), but prime opportunities to exercise his song-and-dance chops were in notably short supply. Until *Hairspray*.

Having accepted the challenge, Travolta focused his formidable talents and energy on creating an interpretation of Edna that worked for this script and its director's vision, and on making the difficult musical numbers his own. "John plays her as a very fragile, hurt-inside person who then gets to come out and discover that she's fabulous," says Adam Shankman. "Of course, he brought a really sweet singing voice, and his ability to move. When Edna discovers the joy of going outside again, he put a spring in her step, and she becomes as light as a feather, like a giddy little girl. That's the Edna for this movie."

Travolta's co-stars and crew were astounded by his ability to fully project his character through the confines of prosthetics and makeup. Zac Efron, who plays Link Larkin (*Hairspray*'s version of Danny Zucko) remembers, "it was incredible, how in the character he was. You know, I had a few talks that I thought were with John Travolta. But I actually think they were more with Edna. John took a prosthetic suit and a dress and a wig and makeup and created a living, breathing woman."

Travolta found it exciting to be back in the intensely collaborative world of musical theater and credits his fellow cast members, along with the script, Shankman, and the makeup and costume team for helping him realize the character. "I always make aviation analogies—in this kind of project every choice of clothing, every piece of music, every dance move, every piece of dialogue ... if it's not excellently put together, it doesn't get off the ground. It's everyone at full throttle."

He finds parallels with his signature movie, *Grease*, in how *Hairspray*'s musical numbers are handled. "It's very organic, the transition from dialogue into musical number." Even before having seen all the whole film, he's sure that audiences will find the movie as much fun to watch as it was to make. "The musical numbers are fabulous. They're as good as any I've ever seen for entertainment value and dazzle."

Hair-Hopper Central

If there's a dream job in the movies for a hair designer, it's got to be *Hairspray*. On her first look through the script, says Judi Cooper-Sealy, "I got so incredibly excited—what an opportunity to prove what you can do, with such a wide variety of looks. All different and fun and interesting and extreme."

"The sixties was a huge period for hair, literally and otherwise," she notes. "People really did concentrate on their hair. Women would go to salons and get it done, and they might keep that do for a week—not like today's wash and wear hair.

"You think of the beehive in particular, really high and narrow hairdos. But the flip was also very popular. Another big look was everything pulled back with lots of curls on top. Or hair worn down but still big and curly, very fussy. Before that, in the fifties, hair was a lot smaller and neater, without so much variety—usually just a French twist or worn back and waved."

Cooper-Sealy had worked with Adam Shankman on *Cheaper by the Dozen 2* and on *Chicago*, and designed hair for Christopher Guest's mockumentaries. Her passion is interpreting characters through hair—"character actors and comedians especially seem to appreciate what I do," she says. Her initial tasks were getting familiar with *Hairspray*'s characters along with lots of research. Absorbing the director's ideas is primary, and Shankman came to an early meeting with very specific ones. "I took notes on all the characters," she says, "then went home and made up a book with several different looks for each. I gave Adam a box of gold stars and told him to stick stars next to the ones he liked."

They started from the premise that most styles would be less extreme than in the stage show. "Mainly I just wanted them to look like people might look in that period," she says. "If you do that, you can have the main characters stand out a bit more."

Changes in hairstyle and costume were used to depict character evolution, especially for Tracy. "We start her out with the flip, very cute and bouncy, almost a caricature of the period," says Cooper-Sealy. Sometimes the look was script-driven: "In the school scene, it had to be teased really high so the kid behind her couldn't see over it." Later, in her excitement at being chosen for the TV show, Tracy gets carried away and bleaches big streaks in her hair. "And near the end of the movie, she gets straight hair, as if she's looking ahead to later in the sixties. The hairdos are meant to go with her growth as a character."

Hair also had to match the mood and physical demands of a scene or musical number, so some of the women had as many as four or five different looks. "I don't like rules," says Cooper-Sealy, "so when I create a character's hair, I always try to do something a little unexpected." With the Dynamites girl group, for example, each girl had basically the same style but the designer used color to differentiate them. "If hair is all dark, it doesn't catch the light as well. So although color wasn't really used much in that period, for the Dynamites I put a slight sheen of purple on one girl, blue on another, and bronze on the third. It's not obvious, but it catches the light."

Another unexpected choice was to make Motormouth Maybelle a blonde. "I felt she had to be kind of bigger than life," says the designer. "So why not a blonde?" Shankman liked the idea. Queen Latifah wasn't sure at first, but once she started trying on wigs, she quickly signed on. "Since we already had some cool, ivory blondes with Velma and Amber, I used a warmer gold on Maybelle," Cooper-Sealy explains.

Maybelle wound up with five different hairstyles. "She's such an interesting character. In some ways she was maternal. In the protest march, I didn't want her to look too glamorous because it was a serious situation. But at other times, we went all out: big, blonde and beautiful hair. Sometimes with curls on the top. And then a sculpted beehive we called the 'Nefertiti.' The look would change according to what she was doing."

For the female leads, Cooper-Sealy relied mainly on wigs, except for Penny Pingleton, whose oddball 'do was a blend of her own hair and extensions. Of the male leads, only Christopher Walken had a wig, and he was adamant that it not look too extreme or different from his natural color and hairline. In fact, the men in general proved more resistant than the women to any radical departure from their usual look.

"Zac Efron had his longish, teenage-idol, surfer hair, but to give him that dramatic look of the sixties, we had to cut and color it." At first the actor protested the loss of his trademark style, but he came around in the end. "His hair's short and very dark brown. With the sixties clothes, the very narrow suits, he looks gorgeous."

On the character of Seaweed, Cooper-Sealy envisioned straightened, processed, wavy hair, which hip young African-Americans once took pains to achieve. Elijah Kelley had problems with that—for reasons of both ethnic pride

12 WYZT TELEVISION

Tracy
I'm all for integration. It's the new frontier!

"Miss Baltimore Crabs"

You can laugh but life's a test
Don't do that, don't do this,
Remember, Mother knows best
for the crown's still in the vault
from when I won "Miss Baltimore Crabs"

A tycoon I wed so cuddly and funny
The old fart dropped dead but left tons of money
Now I run this station

and possible damage to his hair. Cooper-Sealy sympathized: "For whatever reasons, Nat King Cole and other black people of that time thought they had to have soft hair like white people. Thank God they got past that. But it was right for our character." It took the director stepping in to persuade Kelley, but he made the most of his new look.

For the young dancers—the Corny Council Kids and Detention Kids—the challenge was hair that could withstand lots of movement. "When you're doing a film with dancers, you either have to set hair well so that it will come back together, or spray it really firmly, which I don't like to do," says Cooper-Sealy. "If there's movement in the body, you want movement in the hair." So the dancers' hair was set so that it would keep its shape on top but move at the bottom if they shook their heads or turned upside-down. One exception was Amber: "Her hair was always quite neat and didn't move a lot. But that was her personality, too."

The dancers' do's required endless touching up on the set during breaks—just one detail of the vast logistics of designing hair for a film with a large principal cast, some 300 dancers, and hundreds of extras. Some of Cooper-Sealy's staff needed training in back-combing technique: "A lot of newer hairdressers have never done it before." When there were big scenes to prepare, she would stock the extras' trailer with hundreds of wigs, as well as reference boards showing all the possible styles she wanted represented in the crowd. And the stylists would go to work. "I'd tell them, if someone has hair you can work with and do a great sixties look quickly, do their hair. If not, grab some wigs and start trying them on."

During her research, Cooper-Sealy recalls thinking, "I could hardly believe it—they really did wear that towering hair and those crazy things. But that's the fun of making a movie like this. You get to show people what was actually going on." She was also thrilled and inspired by the movie's dancing. "It conveys the feeling of the sixties but is very sophisticated choreography. I wanted do something to enhance how beautiful it is to watch."

Do You Remember...?
Jackie Kennedy's Bouffant

The former First Lady didn't premiere the pouffy style she wore in the early sixties—women's hair was starting to swell by the late fifties. But as with other aspects of her style (the pillbox hat, A-line skirts and uncluttered shapes), Jackie brought the bouffant into the fashion mainstream. As many women remember, the style took a lot of work: setting the hair in huge rollers, often 20 or more, spraying followed by vigorous teasing, then brushing the top layer into a smooth barrel or bubble shape (and more spray). Jackie varied her look: sometimes a flip (or half a flip), more often a page boy (in front of or behind the ears). With bangs or off the forehead. Sometimes an isolated bubble of hair on the top, with wide wings to the side. Now and then an up-do for big occasions. The bouffant probably peaked around 1965, then gradually fell out of favor as the more relaxed late sixties swept in.

"Early in the movie when Tracy gets out of bed, she starts getting ready for the day and back-combing her hair. And spray, spray, spray. How can we create this huge cloud of hairspray around her? At first they tried water, and I said, 'No, no, no. Water would flatten the hair.' Then they tried smoke. We ended up with a spray deodorant, which was white. Backstage, of course, we went through so much hairspray—cases of the stuff. Hairdressers were running out of the trailers saying, 'I can't breathe!'"
— Hair designer Judi Cooper-Sealy

Top row, left to right: Tracy's two looks, Maybelle in big curls, Council girl Shelley, and Amber's teased-up flip. Bottom row: Corny Collins's slicked-back style, Penny's high-top with curls, and Seaweed in his processed waves.

*T*racy and other dance-show hopefuls wait in line at the TV station. Amber gives them — especially Tracy — the haughty treatment, but Link graciously signs their autograph books. As the auditionees file inside, Velma is drilling the Council girls on their steps, censoring any suggestive moves. We learn more than we ever wanted to know about Velma as she reminisces in song and dance about her reign as "*Miss Baltimore Crabs*" of 1947 ... and what she did to win her crown of claws. The scene spins off into fantasy, then back to the present as Tracy is ousted from the audition, just as viciously as Edna feared. Another would-be Council dancer is Little Inez, a 13-year-old black girl with great moves. But, no surprise, she gets dismissed even more rudely than Tracy.

"A movie's only as good as its villain," claims Adam Shankman. Audiences will be happy to hiss at Velma Von Tussle, the scheming, racially bigoted control freak who runs TV station WYZT. But they'll also be enjoying her terrific singing and dancing, her way with a sharp line, and her general gorgeousness, because Velma is played by the one and only Michelle Pfeiffer, in one of her first roles following a family-oriented hiatus from moviemaking.

"When we thought about the character, we thought of her right away," says Neil Meron. "I mean, Velma is an ex-beauty queen, and there's no more beautiful woman in the world than Michelle Pfeiffer. She demonstrated how well she sings in *The Fabulous Baker Boys*. But I don't think she's ever had a role quite like this. She wanted to be stretched, and the material told her that she was going have a good time, be able to sing and dance, and portray a character she can have some fun with.

"So she met with us, read the script, and climbed on board. Climbed into those Velma clothes and heels. And she tears it up." Craig Zadan emphasizes Pfeiffer's gift for comedy: "We remembered how delicious she was in *Married to the Mob*. So that really completed the picture."

Says Shankman: "I just loved the idea of having a woman who looks like that playing such an awful person. Velma's a girl who won a beauty contest and then stopped growing as a person. She needs to win at any cost. And she does not like change. Michelle took on this very daunting task of playing the villain with a real stylish energy, and she was perfect. Even I wasn't prepared for the creature she created on camera."

Pfeiffer admits to some initial reluctance to take on such an unsympathetic character. "I approached every scene trying to humanize her, and sometimes it just wasn't possible." But she always welcomed the challenge of the musical numbers. "I really didn't do any dancing in *Baker Boys*. And I have to say this singing was harder than any I've done before. The melodies are so fast you can barely get a breath in. But once I got past the 'Oh my God, what have I gotten myself into?' phase, it was so much fun to sing again."

Her number also called for baton twirling as part of her pageant flashback. She'd had a little prior experience, but "having to think about singing, dance moves, and on top of that twirling the baton was really pushing the limits of how much I could concentrate on at one time."

Pfeiffer undertook two months of vocal training before she came to rehearse, record, and shoot on location. During rehearsals she would travel to Toronto to run through the "Miss Baltimore Crabs" number. She credits Shankman with making her comfortable in the part and not letting her take it too seriously. "He is very collaborative yet always gives you a sense that he has the bigger picture in mind. He was great about making sure we had enough rehearsal and were comfortable with the staging. But whenever I would get too actory and question my 'motivation,' he would say, 'Honey! It's vaudeville!' That would always put me in my place."

She loved working with the young cast and dancers, who inspired her to give her utmost, and bonded closely with Brittany Snow, who plays her daughter Amber. "My only regret is that we didn't have more scenes together." Her young co-stars in turn were thrilled and at the outset a little nervous to be performing with a screen idol. "When they said it was going to be Michelle Pfeiffer, I probably had a heart attack," says Snow. "I respect her so much: her career and her choices. But she's been so warm and loving, and we have a great relationship. I love watching her work, and I've learned so much from her. It's so refreshing to see somebody at the top of her career still put in so much effort. She wants to make sure everything is perfect: every line, every dance step, every song, every note."

"I have to say this singing was harder than any I've done before. The melodies are so fast you can barely get a breath in. But once I got past the 'Oh my God, what have I gotten myself into' phase, it was so much fun to sing again."
— *Michelle Pfeiffer*

Velma
On my show you'll never find a thrusting hip or bump and grind.

"It's great watching Michelle turn it on. And she's so professional. At one point in the fantasy number I actually get to lift her up!"
— Zac Efron

Costuming the Characters

With a background that includes costuming Broadway musicals and major movies such as *Casino*, *Apollo 13*, *Wag the Dog*, *How the Grinch Stole Christmas* and *A Beautiful Mind*, costume designer Rita Ryack was ideally fitted to dress *Hairspray*. Besides, she says, "I've been obsessed with musical theater since I was four. And I lived the period, I'm sorry to say! It was all happening when I was just becoming aware of music and politics and being kind of a misfit."

Ryack "fought like a cat to get this job," she claims. "For one thing, I love John Waters. The first time I saw a Waters movie I just felt validated. Here was somebody who could take anarchy and put it out there in living color and was just fearless about it."

She and Adam Shankman had similar ideas about how the film's heightened realism would translate into clothing. Their approach was to freely adapt period styles in ways that help identify individuals and groups of characters, make featured players stand out, and reinforce character arcs. "Clothes help tell the story and define the characters," says Ryack. "Costume designers present characters visually so that when you see a person onscreen, you know what that person's about from all kinds of visual cues. From a necktie to the emotional tones of colors to the choice of silhouette—those details help make the character accessible to the audience."

One of her main tools is color. "For the Council girls, for example, we have our sherbet palette. It evokes the way you feel when you look in a bakery window: ice cream and candy and powder puffs, and lipstick colors I remember from *Seventeen* magazine. It was the white lipstick time. The boys' palette is darker and shiny."

For Baltimore and the more downscale characters Ryack used an earthier palette. "Also for the Detention Kids, who are in avocados and golds and rusts." Individual characters sometimes had color cues as well. Velma is a creature of extremes, which the colors reflect. She starts out with "a very icy palette but we moved to using much hotter colors. Her red dresses and bright acidic colors have an emotional impact and set her apart as the wicked queen. She also has the highest heels, the pointiest shoes. Edges and geometry."

Clothing shapes were guided by the period, character profile, and what the performer had to do in costume—dancing, for instance. "You listen to the music, you watch the dancing, how it feels. You think about what the camera

will pick up and appreciate. Which fabric will have enough definition and enough dimension. How about feathers for this number because they move a certain way? Or ruffles for another because of how they move? How about sequins because they reflect light in a certain way?"

The women's looks were a blend of fifties and sixties silhouettes; Ryack points out that the full-skirted "New Look" was still being worn in the early 1960s, and she dressed the Council girls this way. "That postwar retrograde thing that happened to women, when suddenly they were at home, corseted and made up and pushed up. I love the female silhouette from that period, but it was constricting." The Council girls are a bit repressed and behind the times, so "all the dresses have crinolines, and Amber's are more exaggerated. We've changed their bodies by cinching in their waists and doing that pointy bra look. With full skirts and petticoats."

Skirts became straighter and tighter in the early sixties, but Ryack could rarely use this look because of dancing requirements. "Except for the Dynamites, who are in very tight dresses with slits. One of the exciting things about this time was that black recording artists were finally moving into the mainstream." The Dynamites symbolize that moment, in their tight shiny dresses and high heels. "They're very sexy and beautiful."

The men's looks were mostly period-true with a strong Baltimore flavor. "The urban thing was coming into fashion: slim, three-button jacket, short tight pants. There was an Ivy League, JFK, Brooks Brothers way to do it. Then there was the Baltimore way: skinnier lapels and ties, pointier shoes. It's a little more flamboyant. And shiny, shiny fabrics." It was quite a shock for the young actors, she notes, to have real waists. "Especially these kids from the hip-hop generation who are used to these oversized clothes and their pants falling off."

Tracy's clothes are more character-driven. "I think Tracy's already a movie icon in that white blouse," Ryack says. "I could never think of her look without referring back to the original film. White blouses and skirts. Simple, urban and inexpensive. The plaids in her skirts don't necessarily match. You have to think: where would these people shop? What would their resources be? And we assume that Edna, being a laundress, also sews." By the end of the movie, Tracy is in an outfit much closer to the later sixties, a shift dress with an unconstructed silhouette. "No more waist cinchers and girdles and horrible foundations. This

These pages and overleaf: Fabric swatches, sketches by costume designer Rita Ryack, and photographs of some of the outstanding costumes.

last look was not present yet in 1962, except maybe in Paris, but we're showing the freedom that lies in the future."

Actors invariably contribute their feelings about their characters, says Ryack, along with their individual physiologies. "Take Chris Walken playing Wilbur. How different would he be from a shorter, more rotund Wilbur or a lighter-hearted Wilbur?"

John Travolta had strong ideas about Edna's looks, and the prosthetics also imposed some costuming restrictions: necklines couldn't be too low, and short sleeves were out for the most part. "An actor like John is very smart about how he wants to portray the character. He wanted to show his body shape all the time, not cover that up or add excess bulk—which was also a matter of comfort. At the beginning of the story that meant no distracting prints or patterns. We wanted to keep things very simple while she's still in the house." Later, after Edna and Tracy visit the Hefty Hideaway, Edna's costumes change radically: they leave the shop in matching iridescent pink sequins. Then there's the "breakaway" dress Edna wears in the finale. "Adam and I fell in love with some red sequined fabric I'd found. I had the fringe made in India, and that was the Tina Turner dress."

Symbolism figured strongly in Queen Latifah's costumes as Maybelle. Ryack calls her "a funky diva and the moral center of the movie. She's the great mother for all these kids, a very independent spirit. And she's a musician." Maybelle's costumes are less reality-based than others in the film, Ryack feels. "They are about expressing her differences and her sense of personal freedom." Some have an earthy look, like the leopard-print outfit early in the movie. "We wanted very supple fabric that moved fluidly with her. Even the gold and feathers she wears at the end really move when

she walks around. We also used bright colors and a few ethnic touches, like the jewelry."

The costume designer's job, says Ryack, combines design and storytelling skills, as well as intense collaboration. "To make each frame a painting, you're collaborating with the production designer and the cinematographer. It's painting. It's psychology. Of course, you have to have a great knowledge of construction and fabric. Even managerial skills come into play."

And in no small way, to provide costumes for such a large production. The work starts with research on a vast scale: in books, films, magazines, catalogs, high-school yearbooks, as well as in the stocks of industry costume houses. There are infinite choices to be made about sourcing vintage or rented costumes versus building from scratch. "You don't want to see the same garments from film to film, and that's often a problem with renting, especially with men's suits. So I try to track down as much new vintage as I can. Or just build them, as with Corny's outfits." And with multiple costumes for all the featured players, plus dressing hundreds of extras, Ryack had to recruit and direct a wardrobe staff, who worked long hours to organize, maintain and repair costumes during rehearsals and shooting.

Ultimately it's the unique Ryack touch that sets *Hairspray's* costumes apart, so they enhance characterization without taking over. "I just have a very specific point of view," she says. "It's something a bit akin to John Waters, I'd say. Plus a little Diane Arbus, a little musical comedy, a little Dr. Seuss, and a lot of sixties *Mad* magazine.

"I more or less design everything in my films the way I would a musical. You've got your foreground, middle-ground and background characters. The foreground characters are the protagonists, and they have to pop."

Tracy pays a price for cutting class to make the audition: Miss Wimsey sends her to detention. But this turns out to be a gift in disguise. In the detention room she finds a bunch of black kids passing the time practicing new dances to music from a tinny transistor radio. Tracy admires the moves of one Seaweed J. Stubbs, but this earns her no points ... until she demonstrates that she can do them with just as much style. "Not bad for a white chick," he admits — and a friendship is forged. Tracy remembers that Seaweed has danced on The Corny Collins Show, and she starts to wonder why every day can't be Negro Day. As they dance up a storm, they're spotted through the window by Link Larkin. Truly impressed, he tells Tracy that Corny is hosting a hop at the school the next night. And "maybe if he saw you dance like that, he'd put you on the show." Link's compliment sends Tracy off in a happy haze of first love and anticipation. "I Can Hear the Bells," she sings, floating through the school corridors, the nurse's office, teachers' lounge, driver's ed class, music room, and the gym. Even taking a hard whack in dodgeball can't bring this hairhopper down off her cloud.

"I Can Hear the Bells"

Can't 'cha hear my heartbeat
keeping perfect time?

Everybody says
that a guy who's such a gem
won't look my way,
but the laugh's on them

Everybody warns that he
won't like what he'll see
But I know that he'll look
inside of me
Yeah, I can hear the bells...

One little touch

Seaweed
Girl, you ain't just
happening, you have happened!

Hairspray  74 *Part Two*

Let's Twist Again
Dances of the Early Sixties

Rock 'n' roll and its godfather, rhythm and blues, were dance music from their earliest roots. *American Bandstand* popularized the lindy hop in the mid-fifties, but the early 1960s saw the real explosion of rock 'n' roll dance fads, thanks largely to Chubby Checker's tireless promotion of the Twist (and his associated records) on *Bandstand* and on radio. The Twist was easy to learn and caught on fast across society: by late 1961, jet-setters were twisting the night away at New York's Peppermint Lounge. But so were preteen girls at slumber parties with their record players and 45s. Many more dances followed—both short-lived novelties like the Hitch-Hike and classic moves like the Pony. Dances linked with hit records from 1961–63 include: "Mashed Potatoes," "Do You Know How to Twist?," "El Watusi," "The Madison," "Dance the Mess Around," "The Bristol Stomp," "Pony Time," "Hitch-Hike," "Mickey's Monkey," "Hully Gully," "Do the Bird," and "Loco-Motion." For the most of the young *Hairspray* cast, this was all ancient history, but James Marsden got John Travolta talking one day about doing the old dances. "Oh yeah, there was the Twist," said the dance-movie icon, "and then if you got really crazy, the Peppermint Twist. Everything had to have a name."

Tracy
I wish every day were Negro Day.

Seaweed
At our house it is.

"Zac Efron is arguably the biggest male teen heartthrob in the world right now," says Adam Shankman. "So to have a very sweet teen heartthrob—who can sing and dance—playing a very sweet teen heartthrob … how hard is that one to figure out?"

Casting Link Larkin was put off until the part of Tracy had been decided, because the couple had to match up well. "Once we had the Tracy of our dreams, Nikki Blonsky, we thought Zac would be perfect," Neil Meron relates. He was the right age, the right size, the same kind of fresh and youthful presence. And, as casting director David Rubin notes, "Not many teen idols except those that are already pop stars can sing and dance and act."

The timing was perfect for Zac Efron to play Link. His starring role as Troy Bolton in Disney's smash TV movie *High School Musical* had catapulted him onto magazine covers and into the hearts of girls everywhere. A huge fan of musicals, he was hoping for another when *Hairspray* came calling. He sees parallels with *High School Musical* in playing Link, but even more so with the John Travolta/Danny Zucko role in *Grease*. "It's fun to play the cool guy," he says, "and this is a pre-established character, which is something I never got to do before. It's been done in the first movie, it's been done on Broadway. This was my opportunity to see if I could bring anything new and interesting to it."

It's an off-kilter love story, Efron admits: the cool guy falling for the chubby girl. But to him it made sense. "She's got qualities Link would love to have. Her self-confidence, her sense of humor. She's so comfortable with who she is. And Link isn't, in spite of his perfect hair, the nice clothes. He falls in love with her qualities and eventually gives into these feelings. And it's a great decision."

Getting the part was one thing; pulling it off was another. "Since I came straight from *High School Musical*, I think everyone was expecting me to be a great dancer. But I really have very little dance training. I probably had to work harder on the dancing than anybody here." That meant starting to learn his numbers in L.A. before rehearsals even began, then two months of rehearsals in Toronto with Shankman and his assistant. "We'd get up, we'd show up to the stages. And dance all day."

To master the Elvis moves he needed for his "Ladies Choice" number, "I spent many nights in front of YouTube watching Elvis clips over and over, trying to perfect little things he did. The head moves, the little shoulder moves and hip thrusts. You look at those clips and realize why Elvis will never be forgotten."

Efron thinks he understands why musicals reach people so deeply. "Music, I think, amplifies what somebody can feel. There's only so much you can say in dialogue, but if a character can sing a song about what he's feeling, he can directly speak to the audience," he explains. "There's just an amazing feeling when you watch these movies and people simultaneously break into song and dance in a brilliant finale number. All the characters come together and everyone's conflicts resolve in that moment. You genuinely fall in love with those characters. And there's a happiness. I can't really explain it."

"That's the great thing about musicals. When two characters get to dance and sing to each other on screen, there's a level of connection that can't be reached by regular dialogue."

— Zac Efron

Seaweed
Are you crazy? You gotta dance wit' your crowd, and I gotta dance wit' mine.

Record hop! Link sings an up-tempo Elvis-style number, "Ladies Choice," and the dancers get going. Coming in, Tracy and Penny can't help noticing that a long velvet rope splits the gym in two, with white kids on one side and black kids on the other. Tracy spots Seaweed and proposes they do the dance he taught her in detention. He reminds her they can't do it together but tells her to "borrow" the dance—and she whirls off, working her way to the front of the pack, with Corny paying serious attention. ... Penny sees what's happening and dashes off to Tracy's house. She drags Edna and Wilbur to the TV and makes them watch as Tracy dances to Corny's reprise of "The Nicest Kids in Town." "To think I almost stopped her reaching for the stars!" Edna marvels, as Corny presents Tracy as the newest Council member ... and a contestant in the "Miss Teenage Hairspray" contest. This is the last straw for Velma and Amber. They've watched in horror as Tracy declares that if she were the first woman president, "I'd make every day Negro Day." The show's sponsor, Mr. Spritzer of Ultra-Clutch, is also livid, telling Velma "I want that chubby communist girl off the show!" As the hop ends, Corny and Velma are again locked in combat over the show's future.

"The songwriters decided to give Link a cool, upbeat, Elvis-style number, and it's the perfect time for it in the movie. 'Ladies Choice' establishes the connection between Tracy and Link. And it's the kind of number you need in a sixties musical: the rock 'n' roll band at the record hop, with bright colors and backup singers."

— Zac Efron

"Ladies Choice"

Hey, little girl, with the cash to burn
I'm selling something you won't return ...
Once you've browsed through the whole selection
Shake your hips in my direction

Do You Remember...?
John Glenn in Orbit

"If you think I believe he's really up there…!" scoffs Edna, who is sure that manned space flight is being faked for TV. But it's 1962, the year John Glenn became the first American astronaut to orbit the earth. Glenn's Mercury 6 spacecraft, *Friendship 7*, was launched from Cape Canaveral (later Cape Kennedy), Florida, on February 20. During the four-hour-and-55-minute flight, he made three complete orbits, traveling 75,679 miles. Legendary news anchor Walter Cronkite recalled the event 40 years later: "It was a time," he wrote, of "deep American anxieties over where we stood in the race with Russian science. Those of you too young to remember these nervous Cold War days may rightly wonder — what could have possibly frightened us so much us about a country that barely had a working telephone system?"

Edna
I've read all about it, and it's a big fake from some Hollywood set! If you think I believe he's really up there…

Brittany Snow
as Amber Von Tussle

When Brittany Snow heard from Adam Shankman (her director in *The Pacifier* in 2005) that his next project was *Hairspray*, she practically begged to be cast. Shankman warned her that their friendship wouldn't count, says Snow. "Boy, did I have to work for it." Coming in to audition for the part of Amber, says producer Craig Zadan, "she nailed it." With her classic blond beauty, she and her "mother," Michelle Pfeiffer, could pass for mother and daughter—an unexpected bonus.

Snow had already time-traveled back to the sixties for her best-known role to date, Meg Prior in the NBC-TV series *American Dreams*. She's fascinated by the fashions and fads of the period, "how everything's very pastel and pretty, you know? Even the guys, they're pretty." And she loved Amber's wardrobe of frilly full skirts and pearls. "Everyone then was really concerned with each little detail of their look," she says. "And everything was inspired by what was going on in the music."

Amber isn't a lovable girl, but Snow enjoyed the fun of playing the ice princess and the challenge of finding her humanity. "I love getting to slip into this over-the-top character every day. She's trying too hard, obviously, but she's not really nasty, just spoiled and bratty. She's grown up with the image her mother put into her head: of how women should be, how to get what you want by acting like you deserve it all." Amber does have a moment of rebellion, adding some dirty-dancing moves during auditions. "She's done the routine a million times. Her mom probably makes her practice alone in her bedroom at two in the morning. So she makes up something her mom would never approve of."

Amber gets mad when her boyfriend falls for Tracy, but that's more about image than love, Snow thinks. "Link is almost her accessory, like a really great bag. He gets to be famous because he's dating her. They don't really like each other, but it looks good. Lots of relationships are like that, especially in high school: you want to be with the most popular guy because you're the most popular girl."

Like the other young stars, Snow had to work hard on her dancing. Though she had sung and danced since age six, her TV career cut that short, so she started voice and dance lessons again. The best part of *Hairspray*, says Snow, was her friendships with co-stars Nikki Blonsky, Zac Efron, Amanda Bynes, and Elijah Kelley. "We bonded while we were rehearsing—that was really important." They're happy to return the compliment. Says Blonsky: "Brittany has made this experience so much fun for me. She has taught me more than she'll ever know, and I really look up to her."

Snow did them proud, says producer Neil Meron: "We'd known Brittany from *American Dreams* and her incredible character work on shows like *Nip/Tuck*. She's an emerging movie star, and *Hairspray* shows another level of her talent. She's beautiful, has amazing comic chops, and is a really hard worker." Adds Adam Shankman, "She just milks every funny moment out of that character. It was great to watch it unfold."

Maybelle
I'm Motormouth Maybelle, remindin'
you next Tuesday's your rhythm
and blues day — Negro Day will be
comin' your way ...

Overnight, Tracy becomes a star. Every kid in school is her new best friend. Fans all over Baltimore call in their votes for Miss Teenage Hairspray, and Tracy's total is quickly catching up to Amber's. She's even made detention the cool place to be. On her next visit there, she brings Penny along ... and when Penny meets Seaweed's eyes, it looks like the start of something hot. As these scenes unfold, Amber and two other Councilettes begin a new girl-group number, *"New Girl in Town"* ("She's the kitten that the cats prefer") in mocking tribute to Tracy. But then we hear the song again, and it sounds way better as sung by a trio of gorgeous black women: the Dynamites! It's Negro Day, and Maybelle's introducing her latest discovery. Velma is outraged that they're doing Amber's song, but the Dynamites have every right to: they wrote it. To cap Velma's frustration, Mr. Spritzer now is crazy about Tracy because she's boosting hairspray sales.

"New Girl in Town"

The new girl in town
seems to dance on air
The new girl in town
has the coolest hair!

The new girl in town
has my guy on a string
The new girl in town
Hey, look — she's wearing his ring

"'New Girl in Town' was written for the Broadway show, though it was never used. But perfectly it served the film's needs to underscore a montage I did of Tracy's rise to stardom."

—Screenwriter Leslie Dixon

3. RON...

4. "LEADER OF THE PAC...

5. "CHAPEL OF LOVE" by THE D...

6. "UP ON THE ROOF" by THE DRIF...

7. "PLEASE MR. POSTMAN" by THE MAR...

8. "LIMBO ROCK" by CHUBBY CHECKER...

9. "RETURN TO SENDER" by ELVIS PRES...

10. "TELSTAR" by THE TORNADOES

"We all know that real talent's going to show if you give it a chance. Here's a song the Dynamites are performing on Negro Day after Velma took it for her daughter to do ... but she couldn't do it the way they did. So Motormouth is proud of the fact that real is real and it's showing."

— *Queen Latifah*

Girl Groups

*H*airspray's songwriters took much of their inspiration from the classic "girl group" sound of the early 1960s, epitomized by groups like the Shirelles, the Crystals, and the Ronettes. Such songs dominated the pop charts during the gap between Fifties rock 'n' roll (after Elvis decamped for the army in 1958) and the British Invasion of 1964. Early girl-group hits, like the Chantals' "Maybe" in 1958, derived from the male doo-wop style, but later a distinctively lush, textured sound emerged on records produced by Phil Spector, Ellie Greenwich and others, who closely controlled the groups and their repertoire. Spector's famous "wall of sound" relied on dense instrumentation underneath the girlish lead vocals and harmonies.

The vocalists were often in their teens, with church gospel-singing backgrounds, and because most were black, it wasn't hard to keep them anonymous—convenient for producers and record labels that might want to swap out different girls for a tour or a recording session. In fact, the Crystals' big hit "Da Doo Ron Ron" was actually by the Blossoms: Spector, who was feuding with the Crystals, paid the Blossoms session rates to record the song, then released it under the name of his better-known group. And it was easier to promote a record if people didn't know the singers were black. The Shangri-Las, a white trio, broke through the publicity barrier with their bad-girl image and story-songs like "Leader of the Pack," and eventually Diana Ross of the Supremes opened the gates for black female pop stars.

Although some girls wrote their own songs, most of the era's hits came from established songwriting teams like Lieber & Stoller or Goffin & King. Among the biggest were the Shirelles' "Will You Love Me Tomorrow" (the first Billboard number-one hit by an all-girl group) and "Dedicated to the One I Love"; the Ronettes' "Be My Baby" and "Walkin' in the Rain"; the Angels' "My Boyfriend's Back"; and the Crystals' "He's a Rebel" and "Then He Kissed Me."

Hairspray pays tribute to girl groups not just on its soundtrack but in a subplot about a group called the Dynamites, presented by Motormouth Maybelle on "Negro Day" at *The Corny Collins Show*. Reflecting historical fact, the Dynamites write a song that gets co-opted by a white trio headed by Amber Von Tussle—but then the Dynamites sing it the way it should sound. "This was a little bit of a tweak on Pat Boone recording 'Tutti Frutti' for white listeners, after Little Richard had already done it brilliantly," says screenwriter Leslie Dixon. "You suddenly see the difference in how the song can be if it's handled with passion and soul."

Right: Tanee McCall, Nadine Ellis and Arike Rice as The Dynamites.

"I could see that they secretly liked you." That's Penny, consoling her best friend Tracy after Tracy gets booted from the *Corny Collins* audition. Penny's a true-blue pal and the classic sidekick role: a shy, eccentric girl with a tyrannical mom. But while Tracy breaks out as a star performer, Penny breaks through even more radically—she falls in love with Seaweed J. Stubbs, who is black, and follows her heart. An interracial couple isn't big news in a movie today, but in 1962, when the story takes place, it was about as socially daring as you could get.

Amanda Bynes has been a rising star since joining the cast of Nickelodeon's *All That* and was nominated for a Cable Ace Award for her work on the show. She's also starred in hit movies including *What A Girl Wants* and *She's the Man*. So it might surprise some that she wanted the costarring role of Penny so badly. But Bynes saw its great comic potential, and beyond that: "I feel lucky to play this character because she goes through the biggest transformation of anyone in *Hairspray*," she says. "In the beginning, she's very uptight, with a crazy mother who doesn't let her do anything. But then she stands up for her friend Tracy, and she falls in love with Seaweed, which was a racy thing to do at that time. She gets an awesome, sexy boyfriend, and she gets to change."

Casting director David Rubin understands and admires her choice: "Amanda is one of a very few teenage stars who can make movies happen, yet I think she realized an opportunity here. Instead of having everything on her shoulders, she gets to spar in a different ring and realized the growth potential of that experience. She is not afraid to be a character. In a culture where girls are so preoccupied with looking a certain way and being the coolest and the most beautiful … she's all that, but she's not afraid to be goofy. She really is a natural comedienne of the Carol Burnett school.

And that's a tough quality to find in contemporary teenage girls."

Bynes, who cut her teeth on musicals before turning to comedy, loved both the John Waters movie and the musical. To prepare for her audition, she memorized the soundtracks and put together her own sixties look. "I went to a vintage store and bought a very ugly oversized plaid skirt and a frumpy shirt and sweater. And had my hair in a weird ponytail to the side."

Adam Shankman recalls: "She wanted it more than anything and was willing to jump through rings of fire for it. For me, passion, buys you everything. She had all the passion plus that beautiful, sweet little face, and I liked that she was taller than everybody. I thought that was really funny."

Bynes loved being transported back in time during the production, and appreciated Penny's unique costumes. "The Council girls have the cinched waist and big skirts; they're all tidy and sprayed and coiffed. But my character isn't like that. She's free-spirited and a little frumpy, so she wears baggy things, which I really like. Except in the last scene, where I have a very glamorous dress—which is fun for a day but it took nine days to shoot the scene!"

She believes the *Hairspray* story "needs to be told again" and predicts that audiences will go for this telling in a big way. "The key to a great movie is that people have to believe. With some movies you're gone within the first five minutes, because it doesn't seem real or grounded. I think within the first five minutes of *Hairspray*, you want to believe, because it has so much joy."

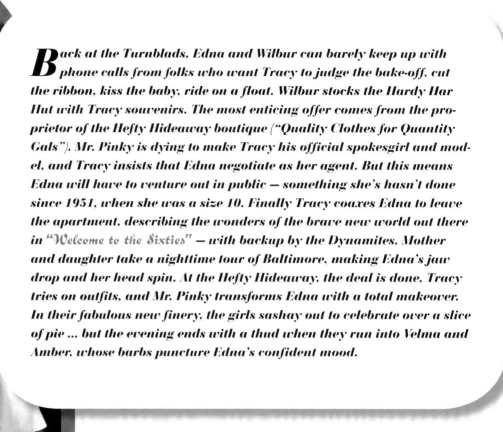

*B*ack at the Turnblads, Edna and Wilbur can barely keep up with phone calls from folks who want Tracy to judge the bake-off, cut the ribbon, kiss the baby, ride on a float. Wilbur stocks the Hardy Har Hut with Tracy souvenirs. The most enticing offer comes from the proprietor of the Hefty Hideaway boutique ("Quality Clothes for Quantity Gals"). Mr. Pinky is dying to make Tracy his official spokesgirl and model, and Tracy insists that Edna negotiate as her agent. But this means Edna will have to venture out in public — something she's hasn't done since 1951, when she was a size 10. Finally Tracy coaxes Edna to leave the apartment, describing the wonders of the brave new world out there in "Welcome to the Sixties" — with backup by the Dynamites. Mother and daughter take a nighttime tour of Baltimore, making Edna's jaw drop and her head spin. At the Hefty Hideaway, the deal is done, Tracy tries on outfits, and Mr. Pinky transforms Edna with a total makeover. In their fabulous new finery, the girls sashay out to celebrate over a slice of pie ... but the evening ends with a thud when they run into Velma and Amber, whose barbs puncture Edna's confident mood.

"It was interesting how readily John went back to his roots in musical comedy. I think his joy in that got him through all the physical stuff he had to bear. And with all the prosthetics, he still moved us. You are emotionally involved with Edna, rooting for her and caring about her."

— *Producer Craig Zadan*

"Welcome to the Sixties"
Hey Mama, hey Mama,
Look around
Everybody's groovin' to a brand-new sound ...

On 1988, he appeared as Wilbur Turnblad in John Waters's original movie of *Hairspray*. That same year, he played Dogberry in a Broadway production of Shakespeare's *Much Ado About Nothing* with Kevin Kline and Blythe Danner—the remarkable span of Jerry Stiller's career in a nutshell. He returns to *Hairspray* (2007) in the cameo role of Mr. Pinky, the dapper owner of the Hefty Hideaway boutique, "which caters to people of girth," as the actor puts it.

Though best-known in recent decades as the hyperventilating Frank Costanza on *Seinfeld*, Stiller first found success in the 1960s, when he and his wife, Anne Meara, were at the top of the comedy game. As the ethnically mismatched team of Stiller & Meara, they appeared on the Ed Sullivan Show (or its predecessor) 36 times. He was also a steady presence on Broadway and TV as a character actor. Though his career sputtered in the 1980s, he still wondered if taking the *Hairspray* job was the right move. "John Waters was a crazy guy, and then there were the items sold in the Hardy Har Hut—different kinds of fake vomit and things you would find on the street. I had just come from doing Great Performances on TV, a production of Saul Bellow's *Seize the Day*, and I thought: image-wise is this what Jerry Stiller wants to project? But my children, Amy and Ben, told me I must do it. And look what happened."

Stiller loved the experience from the moment he met Divine, who played Edna. "There was something about the way he ironed my clothes … I knew right away we were a team, husband and wife." *Hairspray* gave him the chance to relive the sixties, which he missed the first time around. "I had no memory of the sixties. Ann and I were doing our act and trying to make it. And I think I never was a teenager in real life. I never could get the girl." He describes his Brooklyn upbringing as restrictive and says that *Hairspray* "freed up my inhibitions. When you worked with

John you felt you were sixteen again. You were given permission to act silly and adolescent, and not worry about punishment."

If possible, he enjoyed his small part in the latest *Hairspray* even more, marveling at his costumes and wig, the Hefty Hideaway set, the wonderful songs. He appreciates that Mr. Pinky "creates an environment where his customers have nothing to be ashamed of. To him they are beautiful in every possible way." And he even gets to dance: "Just moving the body at this point in life is nice."

Of this movie's Edna, says Stiller, John Travolta "takes over the screen in a very gracious and generous way." Veterans both, the two even did some ad libbing in their big scene. "Edna comes into the shop as her daughter's agent, a little like the mother in *Gypsy*, with a contract to sign. But one thing she wants more than anything is a bustier. When she says 'bustier' my eyes get big. I say '54 double D'? She comes back with '64 D!' And I say, 'I've found the mother lode!'"

The filmmakers, as well as Travolta and Waters, are delighted that Stiller is on the team. Says Neil Meron, "Jerry had more energy and enthusiasm for joining our *Hairspray* family than you could imagine. There he was, close to 80, dancing and acting his heart out at four, five, six in the morning. The entire crew is collapsing around him, but Jerry is still up there saying he's having the time of his life. What a thrill that was for everybody."

Mr. Pinky
There's my shining star! I'm Mr. Pinky. Tracy, is this your older sister?

Mothers and Daughters

I f *Hairspray* is all about family, a major subtheme is mothers and daughters. The movie has four sets of them, and in a light comedic way they suggest the best and worst about that fraught relationship. An effort was made to cast actresses (and one actor!) who could believably pair up, but the production had exceptional luck here. "John as Edna and Nicky as Tracy looked scarily alike," notes Craig Zadan. "And once Brittany Snow is in full hair and makeup, she and Michelle Pfeiffer look exactly like mother and daughter, as Amber and Velma Von Tussle. That's when casting becomes magic." In the third set—Penny and Prudy Pingleton—tall comedienne Amanda Bynes plays the daughter of the tall, infinitely versatile Allison Janney.

When the Amber-Velma team encounters Tracy and Edna in a diner, just a few lines of dialogue establish the contrast in personalities. Both Amber and Velma do nothing but put down their counterparts, while Tracy and her mom take turns trying to make each other feel better.

Costumes were designed to emphasize those contrasts, says Rita Ryack. "First we have Edna and Tracy, who don't necessarily have the best taste in the world. They're working-class, with limited resources. And we assume that Edna, being a laundress, also sews.

"The Von Tussles are always dressed inappropriately over the top. Clearly they have more money than anyone else. It says a lot about Velma and Amber that they would wear mink-trimmed lamé cocktail dresses in the afternoon, while plotting to get Tracy off *The Corny Collins Show*. Mostly they're dressed up in mean, straight silhouettes, and a lot of jewelry. They're really the Barbie Doll characters for me, but they're the most fun.

"Prudy and Penny? That's pretty much speaks for itself. There's Penny dying to bust out. And her uptight moralistic crazy mother who wants to keep her sheltered. It was important that they were buttoned up and in dark colors. Very prudish; nothing to attract attention. Penny's clothes don't define her figure at all until after she's met Seaweed and found herself and her liberation."

The fourth mother-daughter pair? It's Motormouth Maybelle and her daughter Little Inez. These two didn't have as much interaction onscreen as the others, but even so Taylor Parks, who plays Inez, felt the bond. "Queen is kinda like my mom on set," she says. "She's so hilarious and so nice. And Maybelle has that funky attitude, like Little Inez," she laughs. "So we see where she gets it from."

"We wanted to keep Edna's clothing very simple at the beginning of the story, while she's still in the house — until the makeover at Mr. Pinky's, when her confidence is boosted a little bit. Coming out of Mr. Pinky's had to be just, pow, completely different. So we agreed on iridescent pink sequins. Tracy had her little version and Edna had her grownup version."
— Costume designer Rita Ryack

Mr. Pinky's HEFTY Hideaway

MUMU MADNESS!!!

Buy 2 Get 1 FREE!!!

Hey Mama, hey Mama,
Follow me
I know something's in you
that you wanna set free

So let go, go, go
of the past now
Say hello to the love in your heart
Yes, I know that the world's spinning fast now
You've got to get yourself
a brand new start.

Mr. Pinky's HEFTY Hideaway

sale
ON ALL NEW MERCHANDISE

Accessories!
Trousers!
Skirts!
Tops!

Mr. Pinky's
HEFTY
HIDEAWAY

Mr. Pinky's
HEFTY
HIDEAWAY

Mr. Pinky's HEFTY Hideaway

hours

monday	10 - 6
tuesday	10 - 6
wednesday	10 - 6
thursday	10 - 6
friday	10 - 8
saturday	10 - 5
sunday	closed

Edna
Hey, Tracy, hey, baby,
Look at us!
Where is there a team
that's half as fabulous?

Edna's Body Shop

Some of the most intense pre-release curiosity about *Hairspray* centered on how John Travolta would look as Edna Turnblad. Travolta had strong opinions about that himself, as did his director. Creating the complex system of prosthetics and bodysuits that would carry the weight of this transformation was entrusted to special makeup designer Tony Gardner, who was so enthralled by the emerging art and technology of prosthetics that he walked away from college to make it his life's work.

His first assignment, at age 19, was apprenticing with Oscar-winning makeup designer Rick Baker on Michael Jackson's famous video for "Thriller." At Baker's shop he also contributed to *Starman, Harry and the Hendersons* and *Gorillas in the Mist.* With his own company, Alterian Inc., he has designed and created special makeup effects for many productions including *There's Something About Mary, Adaptation, The Spongebob Squarepants Movie,* the two *Jackass* movies, and 2007's *The Shooter* and *Smokin' Aces.* He also worked with Adam Shankman on *Cheaper by the Dozen 2.*

Gardner auditioned for *Hairspray* by making a DVD of "heavy characters" he had created—for example, putting the willowy Gwyneth Paltrow into prosthetics for *Shallow Hal*: "a much more caricatured look than Edna would be," he notes. For ABC-TV, he had built up a 17-year-old girl to go undercover and investigate attitudes about weight in a high school. Perhaps most convincing was a British commercial showing a 400-pound man doing gymnastic floor exercise. "We added a lot of mass onto a real gymnast, along with exposed 'skin'—arms and neckline, all in a tight unitard. He had to execute very strenuous moves—similar to Travolta's dancing challenge in *Hairspray*."

Gardner also impressed the director and producers by bringing up details such as skin texture, hair color, eyebrow shape, and the possibility of the actor's beard showing through after a long day on the set, thereby losing shooting time. Once Travolta's casting was confirmed, "I was thrilled, of course," Gardner says.

Four key criteria had to be met by the special makeup. One, it had to make Travolta look realistically heavy, not cartoonish. Two, it had to make him look unconditionally female. Three, it had to establish Edna's age as "forty-something—we thought she'd be a young mom, if Tracy is around fifteen or so. So Edna would be heavy but not saggy." And fourth, Travolta had to be able to move as if wearing nothing but his own skin. "His hips couldn't be buried; he couldn't be inhibited in any way."

Preproduction work spanned several stages. To start, Gardner collected head shots of Travolta and Alterian artists did designs in Photoshop, altering the actor's features to make them more female but keeping enough to be recognizable. "We considered how much mass to add, what colors worked best with the period makeup, how to deal with hair," he says. Adam Shankman responded to these early ideas, refining directions. "Adam's very articulate as well as visual. He knew what he liked immediately."

Shortly after, Gardner and Alterian project manager Tim Huizing arrived at Travolta's home in Florida with their equipment to do the all-important life-casting: encasing the actor head to toe in plaster bandages for a body cast, and doing an alginate head cast from which fiberglass copies of Travolta would be made. "This gave us head and body forms to build on sculpturally, rather than through the computer," says Gardner.

Several versions of Edna's body were created. Depending on wardrobe for a given scene, they could "assemble" her shape from foam latex arms and legs, silicone-skinned limbs, urethane bodies, or a one-piece bodysuit made of silicone. "Wardrobe designs didn't exist when we were manufacturing, so we had to plan for everything and make lots of variations," says Gardner. As it turned out, Edna occasionally wears sleeveless tops and even underwear, with arms and cleavage exposed. "So we had to use a silicone bodysuit in some cases, though it's harder to maintain and much hotter and heavier for the actor to wear." But because the silicone body parts were made from seamless molds—a technical first for prosthetic bodysuits—the resulting skin texture and color looked smoother and more feminine even under harsh lighting.

During the design process, says Gardner, "we kept refining the character, making the body curvier, the breasts bigger." The bottom line was: it had to be a real woman, but not too exaggerated. "John's over 6 feet tall, so we wanted to counter that by making him very feminine. He talked about a 'bumblebee look'—a big woman encased in tight clothing but still soft and cute." Travolta

also let them know that he tended to gain and lose weight easily, which could change his body structure over the course of a shoot. "He could tell us exactly what four hours of dancing a day would do to his body. So we took that into account."

Designing Edna's facial prosthetics called on the team's every ounce of artistry and craft. About two months before filming, Travolta came in for the first makeup test. "That was the first time he really saw the whole character, complete with wigs," notes Gardner. Travolta's own hair designer, Yolanda Toussieng, came along bearing a dozen wigs, and various combinations were tried out. "At that point it could have gone in many directions. Edna could have been blond, to soften the overall look." How to handle the actor's expressive eyebrows ultimately determined the hair color, with blonde deemed too cartoony. Bangs were added to enhance the "soft and cute" effect.

"Every variable you add affects the overall design—how much of a chin cleft do we keep, how full should the lips be? We ended up throwing away the first sculpted character face after testing it, and starting over," Gardner recalls. "Finally we combined two designs and did a film test on it with John. That one was a go." But they continued to tweak the result even after shooting began. "When Edna would look down hard, the mouth area would 'accordion.' So ten days in we were still resculpting and swapping in new face pieces, still refining the character."

For aesthetic reasons, Gardner decided to use silicone to shape Edna's face. "Foam is the industry standard, but it wasn't subtle enough. Gel-filled silicone is more flexible and translucent—it looks and moves more like real skin. John has great skin, and we wanted to make him younger anyway, just smooth everything out." But the downside was that "silicone is a nightmare to work with. It's slippery and floppy, with no structural integrity. Think of trying to attach raw liver to someone's face."

There were five separate overlapping pieces to the facial prosthetics, so another challenge was making the edges disappear without using heavy makeup tricks. And the silicone tended to move around once the actor began to sweat. "I heat up fast," Travolta warned Gardner, who adds: "So here's a great idea: let's totally encase him in silicone and make him dance really hard—it was the essence of high maintenance."

This ratcheted up the pressure on Team Edna to make quick fixes during rehearsals and shooting, sometimes in mid-shot. "John only had so many hours each day to put together his whole performance—this many for makeup, for rehearsal, for filming. Then he needed 45 minutes just to get out of makeup. And because he was putting so much energy into performing with the prosthetics, he had to be sure to get enough sleep." It was clear that Miss Edna needed a small army to move her through her daily routine efficiently, and Team Edna grew to include Gardner, Toussieng, Steven Prouty, and Margaret Prentice, as well as a personal dresser and an assistant director.

Travolta developed a love-hate relationship with Edna's body. "Designing it all wasn't easy, but wearing it was even harder," he says. "Five hours, sometimes, putting on all the latex. There were individual legs that attached to a torso piece that integrated with arms, zipped up the back and clipped here and buckled there. Over that was a girdle and a cinch, all sorts of apparatus. But I was very happy because on film it worked so well."

Aside from the ever-present temptation to fondle those latex curves, *Hairspray*'s filmmakers hail the accomplishments of Team Edna and their creation. Says Adam Shankman, "Tony Gardner made Edna a real singing, dancing doll. John himself was incredible: lots of people have been made large for film, but most don't have to do hours of dancing and singing." Craig Zadan recalls, "We were frightened that John would come to us at some point and say, 'I can't take this.' But he never expressed that he was uncomfortable or unhappy. It showed what a pro he was.

"It was interesting how readily he went back to his roots in musical comedy. I think his joy in that got him through all the physical stuff he had to bear. And with all the prosthetics, he still moved us. You are emotionally involved with Edna, rooting for her and caring about her. So John's real achievement is to go past the rubber on his face and give an acting performance."

"John's my dream date," Gardner says simply. "He was so committed and just indestructible in his focus. I'd never experienced anything like it and hadn't expected it. You always dream of working on someone and have them be like this. But it's so rare."

DETENTION NOTICE

Devious Amber gets Tracy in trouble at school, so it's another trip to detention. This time Link, who's begun to have strong feelings for Tracy, gets himself sent there too ... take that, Amber! Link can't quite master the dance groove but makes friends anyway. Penny's there, and Seaweed invites the whole gang to a platter party at his mom's store — she's none other than Motormouth Maybelle. The white kids are uncertain but thrilled about visiting a black neighborhood. As they all surge out of school, Seaweed tells the world where it's at in *"Run and Tell That."* Other kids join in, and so does his little sister, Inez, who is a big fan of Tracy's. The song climaxes wildly as they board a bus for the ghetto. Amber, in shock, sees Link with them and reports his defection to Velma ... then tattles to Edna in an anonymous phone call.

report at the end of period _____ or penalty will be _____

tention _____

eacher's signature _____

"Run and Tell That"

I can't see why people look at me
and only see the color of my face

The darker the chocolate
the richer the taste
And that's where it's at ...
Now run and tell that!

And if you come
and see the world I'm from
I bet your heart
...onna feel it too

"'Run and Tell That' was written to have the feel of an early Motown, Wilson Pickett kind of song. I had found a dictionary of black slang that was really helpful to us. We made a list of phrases that jumped out at us, and 'run and tell that' sounded like something Seaweed could use."
— Lyricist Scott Wittman

"When it came time to shoot 'Run and Tell That,' I got a rude awakening. I had never sung and danced it at the same time, outdoors on the grass — just practiced on dance canvas. I was feeling pretty confident, but then the music comes on and I go to do the dance, and pretty soon I was gasping for air...like, what happened? Right there I gained a new respect for every movie musical ever made."

— Elijah Kelley

Seaweed
My mom's having a platter party. You-all wanna come check it out?

Penny
Wow! Being invited places by colored people!

Elijah Kelley
as Seaweed J. Stubbs

"The funny thing is," says Elijah Kelley, "I had to sing "I Know Where I've Been" in high school my senior year. But I didn't know much about *Hairspray*, and never in a million years did I ever think I'd be doing this movie." But Kelley was a unanimous choice to play Seaweed "from the moment he literally burst into the audition," says producer Neil Meron. "He was the very first person we saw for any role, and we stopped looking after that. Not only is he vastly talented, he has a face that lights up in front of the camera."

"For Seaweed, I wanted somebody gorgeous, who could really dance—and dance differently than the white kids," notes Adam Shankman. "Seaweed has big open eyes and a beautiful soul, and he exudes sexual radiance. Elijah has all that, plus he can be very funny." The 19-year-old Kelley's most recent starring roles were in New Line's *Take the Lead* and the independent feature *Heavens Fall* (2006), in addition to many TV credits.

"Seaweed's a fun-loving guy," says Kelley. "He's a romantic, and also kind of a wise guy. Cracks jokes all the time. He'll find the humor in anything." In short, a character who will appeal to audience members of both sexes.

Like the other young stars, Kelley approached the sixties like a foreign land that was a blast to visit. "The guys were smooth then, everything was just so put together," he says. "The way we dress definitely makes you act different. Your swagger changes when you're wearing a skin-tight suit with pointy-toed shoes, a skinny tie, and finger waves. You've got to embody that to make the character."

To hone his period dancing, Kelley went right to the source. "I looked at a lot of groups—the Four Tops, the Temptations, James Brown. I acquired the moves from watching them. Those guys are legendary and still known to this day all over the world. They were so smooth. Even James Brown … he was energetic but still smooth. That's what I wanted to have in my repertoire for this movie."

As a contemporary black actor who happens to be from LaGrange, Georgia, Kelley can be serious (at least briefly) about *Hairspray*'s racial theme. Queen Latifah, who plays Seaweed's mom, helped Kelley feel the power of the protest march scene. "She passed down to me what that march really meant. The first time we did it, it was like, okay, we gotta march, let's get the shot, you know. But then we talked about how this stuff really happened, and people need to remember it and try to embrace the feelings around that situation. And once I did that, it was very powerful. You just don't experience that every day."

Kelley played Seaweed's romantic side to the max opposite his pal Amanda Bynes. Seaweed and Penny have an intense mutual attraction that can't be denied, he says, no matter what stands in the way. "That relationship is so vital and important to the story because they go against the grain." Says Bynes: "Elijah brings so much to the role. He has this old-school vibe and look. To me he just looks like an old-time movie star."

Kelley's big number, "Run and Tell That," is a song with great drive and lyrics that are both heartfelt and provocative. "They gave me a little bit of liberty to explore with the performance, because I couldn't sound like anybody else in the movie with that song," he notes with satisfaction. "It's so full of passion and energy."

Cool School

Among the wonderful exterior locations Toronto provided for the production was the building that became Tracy's high school. "It was one of the first things I went to look at with Adam and the producers," says production designer David Gropman. "It's such a great piece of architecture, designed by a local architect and actually dedicated in 1962, the year our film is set in. So it's period-perfect. It had such a great spirit to it and felt so right for the film, that even though it wasn't Baltimore, it was the Baltimore of *Hairspray*."

He and Shankman knew what they wanted the school interiors to look like from the beginning, Gropman says. "We had excellent research and practical locations to rely on." School spaces included Tracy's classroom, the detention room where so much action takes place, the gym for the record hop, and glimpses of various other locations: a band room, nurse's office, hallway, girls' restroom and teachers' lounge. All were fitted out in such authentic detail by art director Dennis Davenport and set decorator Gordon Sim that baby-boomer audiences will practically be able to smell the chalk dust. "The very first classroom we shot, near the end of the 'I Can Hear the Bells' number—that may be my favorite set on the movie," says Gropman.

At Maybelle's record shop, a party is in full swing as the kids arrive. She launches into a song celebrating her identity as a big, beautiful woman. In a parallel scene, the song "Big, Blonde and Beautiful" is picked up by Velma, who's plotting her revenge on Tracy while getting dressed to kill. Maybelle welcomes the kids, and even Penny starts to relax and give in to Seaweed's charms. Tracy and Link are also getting cozy to the music. It's all bliss ... until the music stops with Edna's dramatic entrance. Aghast at the company Tracy's keeping, she starts to drag her away, but Maybelle intervenes. There's a tempting soul-food spread laid out on tables in the store, and Maybelle sings its praises ("We'll keep it in our oven till it's good and hot") until Edna wavers, then gives in and joins the feast.

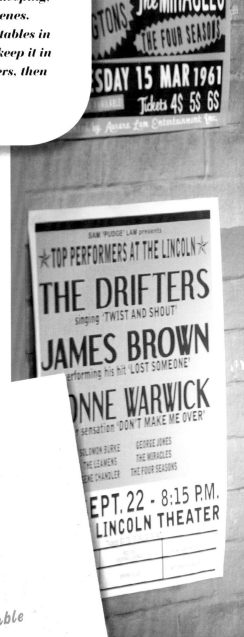

"Big, Blonde and Beautiful"

I offer big love
with no apology
How can I deny the world
the most of me?

Because I'm ...
Big blonde and beautiful
Face the fact — it's simply irrefutable

"For me, it's a chance to let it all hang out. You think you can dance a little bit, then you get around real dancers and you realize, that's dancing. But instead of being intimidated, you've just got to step up and enjoy it. There's a constant energy on the set that's just different from most movies."

— *Queen Latifah*

Once Queen Latifah was safely cast as Motormouth Maybelle, producer Craig Zadan could admit that "there was a list of one. And we had no backup. Who else is African American, the right age, a great singer and actress—and a movie star?" Fortunately Latifah had great experiences working with both the producers (on *Chicago*) and director Adam Shankman (on *Bringing Down the House*).

"They brought the idea of this role to me and explained how important Motormouth is to the changes that happen in the film," the actress recalls. "There was still no script, so I had to bank on Neil and Craig and Adam's expertise. Since we've all worked together before, I felt pretty comfortable. And getting to do a musical is always fun."

She found Maybelle a fascinating, multilayered character to develop. "I see her as a pioneer for her time—somebody that's always been gifted in music and has a gift of gab, knowing how to get connected and be in the right place at the right time," says Latifah.

"She's also a mother who relates well to her kids and knows how to connect with young people in general. My own mom was really my model for that part of her—she was a high school teacher, that cool teacher all the kids would go to when they had some problem. She would inspire them to have sit-ins and do other things that empower kids. I think Motormouth is the same. She sees the youth as the future and lets them know the world is theirs if they want it."

Maybelle's costumes captured her essence, thinks Latifah. "I would call her a superhero, because some of these outfits just remind me of Wonder Woman. They're sexy and soulful at the same time. Then the hair goes up, and I really feel like a superhero."

She theorizes that Maybelle probably made some of her own clothes or bartered for services. "I think women then were much more accustomed to pulling things together and making their way out of no way. So Maybelle could figure out how to get some fabric and maybe get somebody to sew while she did them a favor in the record store. I mean, she didn't get a TV show spot in the sixties by being a passive sort of woman."

Latifah's career is as diverse as any in the movies today, her initial huge success as a hip-hop recording artist followed by a series of major film roles, including *Chicago, Taxi, Beauty Shop, The Last Holiday*, and *Stranger Than Fiction*. A pioneer in her own right, she is also an entrepreneur and label president, and continues to record best-selling albums. "My background is just so all over the place," she notes. "I did high school plays for fun but can't say that I've come from a stage background where I get to sing, dance and act all the time." She appreciates the strong work ethic of stage people, as well as their support and encouragement of her work in *Hairspray*.

"For me, it's a chance to let it all hang out. You think you can dance a little bit, then you get around real dancers and you realize, *that's* dancing. But instead of being intimidated, you've just got to step up and enjoy it. They don't expect you to have 20 years of dance experience. They expect you to do what you do and give it 110 percent. There's a constant energy on the set that's just different from most movies."

If she can identify with Maybelle, Latifah still "can't imagine what it must have been like to really live in that time. All I can do is glance back in books and history that I see through the media." But there have been times on this production, she says, "when you almost feel like you live in a segregated time—when literally the black kids worked at one time and the white kids separately.

"Motormouth has this line, about putting up with Velma: 'It's just a foot in the door.' One step at a time. If you crack the door open, then other people can come in and surpass you and keep positive change happening. There's always stuff to deal with in order to make things change. So, she doesn't just quit and say 'Forget it; I can't take this woman.' She's just knows it's just a matter of time." Maybelle surely would have been proud that someone like Queen Latifah came through the door she cracked open.

Jukebox Jive
Top Hits of 1962

These gems were Billboard #1 hits in 1962, or came close:

"Big Girls Don't Cry"
The Four Seasons
The second of two huge hits by the Jersey boys that year; "Sherry" was the other.

"Breaking Up Is Hard to Do"
Neil Sedaka
Brill Building songwriter Sedaka ("king of the doo-be-doo's") merged his high tenor and tight backup harmonies by the Cookies in this immortal teen anthem.

"Do You Love Me
(Now that I Can Dance)?"
The Contours
Long-lived dance party cut capitalized on dance fads; it was the Motown label's first hit.

"Duke of Earl"
Gene Chandler
Throwback to the doo-wop era, an all-time classic novelty cut.

"Green Onions"
Booker T. & The MG's
The groundbreaking, funky Memphis sound of Stax Records bursts on the scene

"Having a Party"
Sam Cooke
With B-side ballad "Bring It On Home To Me," this disk showcased Cooke's unparalleled vocal gifts.

"He's a Rebel"
The Crystals
Among the greatest girl-group songs, written by Gene Pitney; features Phil Spector's "wall of sound."

"I Can't Stop Loving You"
Ray Charles
Brother Ray makes country his own.

"The Loco-motion"
Little Eva
Standout combination of two genres: girl groups and dance crazes, penned by Goffin & King.

"Peppermint Twist"
Joey Dee & The Starliters
The house band at New York's Peppermint Lounge, the Starlighters had their biggest hit with this Twist spinoff.

"Sheila"
Tommy Roe
Proto-bubble-gum tune transcends the genre with driving tempos and Buddy Holly-type licks.

"Soldier Boy"
The Shirelles
A fave at preteen slumber parties and ladies' choice slow dances; typical sappy girl-group lyrics

"The Wanderer"
Dion & the Belmonts
The apex of male teenage bravado.

Also spending time at #1 in '62: Chubby Checker's "The Twist" (the second time around for this 1960 hit), "Roses Are Red" (Bobby Vinton), "Johnny Angel" (Shelley Fabares) and Connie Francis's "Don't Break the Heart that Loves You," "Good Luck Charm" (lesser Elvis), "Hey Baby!" (Bruce Channel), "Monster Mash" by Bobby "Boris" Pickett, "The Stripper" (David Rose), "Telstar" by the Tornadoes, and one more novelty: "The Lion Sleeps Tonight," by the Tokens.

Hairspray Through the Camera

"The most important thing about shooting *Hairspray*," says director of photography Bojan Bazelli, "was to tell the story through the dancing. There are, I think, twenty-seven dance numbers in the movie, and they communicate a lot of what you need to know about the characters." So how do you shoot people dancing so that their body language reflects what they're trying to express? Where do you put the cameras to capture it all?

Bazelli's credits include *Mr. & Mrs. Smith, The Ring, Kalifornia, Boxing Helena,* and *King of New York,* among many other films. He had never photographed a musical and saw *Hairspray* as a chance to explore a different film language in the service of this story.

To begin with, he found that close-ups were far less important than in other kinds of film storytelling. "The dancers mainly need to be shown in full body. Close-ups don't express much when the bodies are moving so fast. Music videos sometimes get very close to people dancing, but it's usually for a specific, very stylized effect." For most of the dance numbers, Bazelli used several cameras dedicated to medium and wide shots, sometimes with one for tighter views.

Also in the interest of clarity, he used few handheld or steadicam shots—"again, we didn't want any radical camera movement like you see in music videos. The cameras were mostly on dollies, and the camera technique stays in the background." One model they looked to was the classic movie musical *West Side Story,* which broke ground by shooting dance dynamically in outdoor locations, using angles that enhanced the drama but avoiding distracting camera effects.

A key goal of the cinematography was to capture movement in as many dimensions as possible. In some filmed musicals, the movie audience has essentially the same two-dimensional view as a theater audience, but Shankman wanted viewers to see the action from all sides. For example, "in the scenes that take place in the WYZT studio, we shot the action with cameras pointing in opposite directions. You see not just what the TV audience sees, but from the viewpoint of the show's staff."

One challenge on *Hairspray* was that nearly half the film takes place inside that studio, which couldn't simply look like a contemporary soundstage. "In those older studios, the lighting would be very flat," Bazelli explains.

"Though we had to diverge from that a little, we did find some vintage lighting instruments, which are used in these scenes, as well as an old Hollywood TV camera. We looked at black-and-white footage from the sixties, and to suggest that, a scene appears in the monitor of that old camera, in black-and-white, along with the same scene in color, in the main shot."

The principle of shooting from multiple angles carried over to the outdoor sequences such as "Welcome to the Sixties." where you see shots looking up and down the street, and the dancers from above and below.

Lighting and camerawork were critical to keeping the film on that fine line between realism and the "heightened" world of musical comedy. "We're showing an old city, not fancy," Bazelli notes. "But it couldn't look too grim and depressing, because Tracy with her optimism sees something beyond her ordinary neighborhood and street." So the locations were shot to look working-class "but a little bit funny and exaggerated. It's not ultra-naturalistic."

The movie's tonal spectrum reflects the colors and tones of the sixties, he says: "less saturated, paler and softer, more neutral than a lot of what we see today. People are always acting in full light, with just a suggestion of shadows—nothing too deep."

Even in nighttime Baltimore, the lighting was different than it would be for a non-musical film, Bazelli points out. "It has more color, more transparency, not a flat dark like in some films. You need to see costumes, see shadows." It can actually be easier to create a dramatic nighttime effect, he says—but they were after something more subtle, which takes more work.

The camera crew took great pains, especially in the Turnblad apartment set, to avoid the look of interiors that are obviously created on a soundstage. A giveaway is often that that the set is lighted from above, because it's easier that way. "Normally ceilings are removable for shooting, but here we worked with production design to build a box with a fixed seven-foot ceiling, which forced us to be more original and creative in lighting," says Bazelli. "The camera angles often include the ceiling, so it looks like a real location, with light coming only from the windows—or at night from 'practical' lights such as table lamps" (but with stronger bulbs). "It gave a more intimate look than typical studio photography, a sense of real space."

While he started with certain ideas for how scenes should look, Bazelli was constantly adjusting his approach during rehearsals and shooting, often taking

cues from production design and wardrobe. Maybelle's record shop originally was conceived as a dark and smoky club, "sort of beat up and dirty," he says. But that would have been out of sync with the well-dressed and well-groomed people in the scene, so the shop got an upgraded, more stylized look. "The frame must fit the painting," he notes.

While he was often left to come up with ideas for the camerawork on his own, Bazelli received great feedback from producers Zadan and Meron, he says. Their long background in movie musicals gave him confidence in their suggestions, augmenting his collaboration with Shankman.

Basically, he says, they needed to create environments that meshed organically with the comedy writing, singing and dancing. "We had to show the dancers' bodies in the best way, so the dancing looks good, the body language is clear, the emotions come across." The image onscreen must engage the audience, so they're willing to spend two hours getting to know the characters. "And when someone opens their mouth to sing, everything around them should convey that it's a musical," he says. "People should recognize the style as right for the time, right for the stylized musical form, and helping the story move forward."

Maybelle
Time you all knew. Velma Von Tussle just told me that we've had our last show.

Tracy
If we can't dance... maybe we should just march!

Velma descends on the Hardy Har Hut. She exerts herself mightily to seduce the oblivious Wilbur, who only wants to show off his joke merchandise, much to her frustration. ... Back at the record store, Maybelle announces that Velma has abolished Negro Day. This party is a farewell party. Inez is crushed — there goes her chance to dance. It starts to dawn on Tracy that there might be more important things in life than a great hairdo or getting a spot on TV. If she can't dance with her friends on The Corny Collins Show, something has to be done, and she impulsively proposes that they march on the station. Maybelle quickly grasps the possibilities and rallies her neighbors to the idea. But it's a little too much adventure for Link, who is expecting some big-time agents to catch his act at the Miss Teenage Hairspray contest. He exits, with Tracy hiding her pain. Edna tries to comfort her as they head home.

Velma
You don't need those X-ray specs to see what's under these clothes...

There's a certain symmetry to the casting of Walken as Wilbur, observes Adam Shankman. "Wilbur Turnblad owns a novelty shop, and Chris Walken is like a human novelty shop. He's full of quirks and originality."

Walken calls it an accident that he became famous for his dramatic portrayals of menacing or unbalanced characters, since his early background was in musical comedy and TV variety shows. "When I was a kid in the fifties, my brothers and I were in show business. Television shows all came out of New York then, a huge number of live shows every week from the studios around Rockefeller Center. And those shows would use lots of kids almost as set dressing, especially at the holidays."

As a boy, he trained at the Professional Children's School and went on to appear in many stage plays and musicals—in summer stock and touring companies as well as New York. Until nearly age 30, song and dance was the basis of his career. But his dramatic acting soon gained notice, with award-winning performances on Broadway of *The Lion in Winter, The Seagull, The Rose Tattoo*, and other plays.

Walken's New York childhood informed his portrayal of Wilbur in many ways. He understands this man who works downstairs from where he lives. "The way he loves his business reminds me of my father, who had a bakery. He was very good to his family, but I think what he really loved was going to work every day in the bakery, even weekends. Wilbur really loves to go down to the Hardy Har Hut and sell toys.

"I grew up in a part of Queens where a lot of people had their business downstairs and lived upstairs," he adds. "A laundry or grocery or whatever. It's a kind of European immigrant thing. I think that's kind of a perfect life. Wilbur has his family upstairs, and the Taj Mahal of joke shops downstairs. He's a very happy man. I can identify with somebody who loves his work."

Walken also remembers the penny-arcade amusement centers New York was once full of, and their unique atmosphere. "All up and down Broadway were these places on the ground floor of buildings where they'd have games—sometimes pool tables and ping pong, too. There was always a section where they sold joke stuff: whoopee cushions and rubber dog-doo and things that popped out of jars and ice cubes with bugs in them."

Conveying Wilbur's abiding love for Edna was the essence of Walken's task in *Hairspray*. Travolta had asked that Walken play opposite him, because he knew the other actor could play it straight and convincingly. Walken sees it as a match that's simply meant to be. "It's like 'Jack Sprat would eat no fat, and his wife would eat no lean.' They're an inseparable pair. And he's crazy about Edna. He's a man madly in love after many years of marriage."

It was a balancing act, says casting director David Rubin. "There's something vaudevillian about this character, an old-fashioned showbiz quality that's hard to find in the 21st century. Chris has that stage background, yet his performances don't really have tremendous theatricality. Even when he takes a character out there it's never over the top. So he is never commenting on this couple. It was going to be the real deal."

Producer Neil Meron says the relationship is encapsulated in Wilbur and Edna's "Timeless to Me" duet, a highlight of the movie. "John has key dance moments in his career that people identify him with. I think he and Chris Walken have added another image to that incredible legacy."

Walken's work as a dancer didn't end in his youth: many recall with admiration his dance number in the Oscar-nominated *Pennies from Heaven*. In 1988, for Cannon Movie Tales "I did a musical movie of the children's story *Puss in Boots*, though few people saw it." More recently he contributed a mesmerizing dance performance to the Spike Jonze-directed music video for Fatboy Slim's "Weapon of Choice."

When Walken visits New York these days, attending Broadway shows is a top priority, and he hopes that film studios will again make song and dance part of their agenda. "I think if I'd been born maybe 25 years sooner, I might have been in lots of movie musicals," he says. "I've been inspired very much by all the ones I've watched."

Wilbur

Welcome to the Hardy Har Hut! If you can't put a smile on your face, your skin's too tight!

HARDY HAR HUT

"Fun, Jokes & Magic"

WILBUR TURNBLAD
PROPRIETOR

PHONE KL5-0159   BALTIMORE, MARYLAND

HARDY HAR HUT

The "Taj Mahal of joke shops" is Wilbur's workplace but also his refuge. In the way other men might retreat to their den or workshop, Wilbur loves communing with his novelties and gadgets in the safe confines of the shop. It also becomes his bedroom when Edna briefly kicks him out of the house.

The production design team wanted to make it a special place. "It's a major story point that Wilbur owns a joke store," says David Gropman. "The interior of the Hardy Har Hut is a commercial interior. But at the same time it reflects Wilbur's personality.

"For the exterior, I wanted to create something that tells you that it's a joke shop, a place of fun and frivolity. But it had to be believable too, because it's part of a residential building. And because it's the only business on that residential street, we couldn't really let go architecturally. The façade couldn't be too much of a stretch from the nearby exteriors."

The art department created an amazing array of merchandise for the shop—from fake noses and burning cigarettes, vomit and fried eggs, to the classic Groucho glasses, joy buzzer, rubber snake, nail-through-the-hand trick, squirt camera, and countless more items. The store signage's and pictorial ads were all done in period style and typography, based on diligent research. Gropman created certain visual links between the downstairs shop and upstairs apartment, including items from the joke shop that migrated upstairs. "Wilbur's bar in a corner of the apartment is shaped like the prow of a boat and full of stock from the Hardy Har Hut," he notes. "Or there might be a fake fried egg or a bit of plastic barf on a side table."

Wilbur's wardrobe echoes the look of the shop, and he's never without a handy gadget—like the fake lapel flower that squirts water, dousing the candlelight at the end of "Timeless to Me."

Bubba Teeth

Take a set to your next party.

adams'

Fake Nose

Your friends won't recognize you!

GREAT INSTANT

adams'

Crazy Wolf Eyes

POP-OUT EYEBALL GLASSES

They're so much fun!!

Adams'

Pucker Chewing Gum

Flavored with a powerful extract of pure alum.

Adams'

Joy Buzzer

Feels like an electric shock!

Rubber Snake

Scare your friends!

Looks real!

UIRT

mera

adams'

Joke Fried Egg

Fool your friends and family!

LOOKS REAL!

Do You Remember.....?
Milestones of 1962

- **Rock 'n' roll** and its godfather, rhythm and blues, were dance music from Algeria gains independence after 132 years of French rule.

- **JFK** sends federal troops to help register James Meredith, the first black student at the University of Mississippi.

- **Marilyn Monroe** and Eleanor Roosevelt die.

- **The first James Bond** movie, Dr. No, is released, starring Sean Connery with a dripping wet Ursula Andress as Honey Ryder.

- **Pop Art** bursts on the artistic scene.

- **The Beverly Hillbillies** invade TV land.

- **Edward Albee's** scorching *Who's Afraid of Virgina Woolf* opens on Broadway.

- **The Beatles** have their first hit single in England, "Love Me Do."

- **Australian Rod Laver** wins the tennis Grand Slam.

- **Rachel Carson** publishes *Silent Spring*, detailing the hazards of pesticides and promoting a quantum leap in environmental awareness.

- **The aluminum pull-ring tab**, invented by Alcoa, is first marketed by the Pittsburgh Brewing Company.

- **The first discount store chains**, Wal-Mart, Target and K-Mart, all open for business.

- **Telstar**, the first communications satellite, is launched into orbit by AT&T, inspiring a rock 'n' roll instrumental hit.

- **The drug thalidomide** is banned after causing tragic birth defects in the U.S., Canada and West Germany.

- **James Watson**, Francis Crick and Maurice Wilkins win the Nobel Prize for demonstrating the double helix structure of DNA.

- **Pope John XXIII** convenes the Second Vatican Council, liberalizing the Church for millions of Roman Catholics.

*W*ilbur must be working late again, Edna thinks as she sends Tracy to bed. Feeling sexy and good about herself, she takes her turn singing *"Big, Blonde and Beautiful,"* primping while she waits for him to come upstairs. But Wilbur is still in Velma's clutches at the joke shop ... she has to literally fall on top of him to get his attention. And that's exactly how Edna finds them when she goes see what's keeping her husband. ... When Tracy doesn't arrive at the show next day, Corny's worried and suspects Velma is at the bottom of it somehow. Tracy is home making peace between Edna and Wilbur, who's been exiled to the joke shop. As she talks to her dad, she realizes she can't let the Von Tussles win. She'll have to fight for what she believes is right. After she goes to bed, Wilbur ventures upstairs and swears his eternal devotion to Edna. They duet on *"You're Timeless to Me,"* and their drab backyard morphs into a fantasy set with Edna and Wilbur in dance costumes doing a tango, then a ballroom number. As the scene ends, Wilbur squirts out the candle with his lapel flower, and darkness modestly descends.

Backyard Paradise

"**W**hen we came to create the backyard set for 'Timeless to Me,' we knew we wanted to shoot the number on stage," says production designer David Gropman. "It was a complicated piece of choreography, and certainly one of the more emotional and sensitive songs in the film. So being on location seemed the wrong way to go. We needed to be able to control the conditions.

"The big challenge was achieving an absolute sense of reality, so you don't feel like you're in the middle of a stage number. We started with research into working-class backyards in Baltimore at that time. There were wonderful period photographs, as well as extant alleyway backyards to look at."

Gropman had discovered while investigating Baltimore that such backyards typically were small and narrow, facing onto a common alleyway. Chain-link fences separated one yard from the next, sometimes augmented with more decorative or wooden fencing. At the alley end, there was usually a detached garage, "which people would personalize, sometimes using them as workshops.

Maybe there's a curtain in the window, or just an open window into a garage. And there might be a little bit of garden to give it some distinction or privacy."

He photographed many such yards, knowing that the Turnblads' would be the setting for a major production number. And he was pleased to discover that some Toronto neighborhoods contained very similar examples.

All this work went into his designs, which were then translated by his crew on a Toronto soundstage. "You just pay attention to those details. Don't embellish too much. If you do your work well, and have a good construction team and good painters, you can recreate the effect."

The surface underfoot was the final piece, because the number featured so much dancing. "I decided to do a concrete backyard so the actors wouldn't have to get involved in dirt and clumps of grass. The scenic department did a beautiful job making what looks like wonderful old concrete, cracked and parched."

"I thought that Wilbur should be more woven into the plot, not standing on the sidelines so much. So I made him the target of an evil seduction attempt by Velma, which wreaks havoc in the Turnblad household. In a stage musical, characters can be happy all the time, and it's fine. In a movie, everything has to go wrong until it goes right in the very last frame. I wanted there to be some problems in the marriage so that lovely song 'Timeless to Me' could be their reconciliation."

— Screenwriter Leslie Dixon

"Timeless to Me"

Styles keep a-changin'
The world's rearrangin'
But Edna, you're timeless to me . . .

*Fads keep a-fadin'
and Castro's invading
but Wilbur, you're timeless to me . . .*

Storytelling in Song

Integrating songs with the film story is the crux of making a movie musical. Producers Zadan and Meron had forged solid principles from their experience in bringing stage material to the screen, and director Adam Shankman was on the same page. Putting the details on paper was screenwriter Leslie Dixon, who analyzed the source material with a sharp pencil, seeking to identify what would work on film, what had to go, how songs might be treated differently this time, and what action might call for new musical support.

"There's actually quite a bit that's new in the script, but I tried hard to weave it in with the existing songs," Dixon says. How could we work each song into a strong story line, and what purpose it would serve? In a Broadway musical a character can stand up and sing for no particular reason. It just has to be a great song or the right moment for an upbeat number. In a movie I felt it had to connect to the plot."

A look at individual numbers reveals much about the process. The film opens with "Good Morning, Baltimore," introducing Tracy and her world. "Adam has shot the number all over the city," says Zadan, thus immediately breaking through any stage constraints and opening up the canvas. By launching into music at the very top, even before the titles, Shankman intended to establish the logic of musical storytelling throughout. "She wakes up, and the music is already going," he says.

"The Nicest Kids in Town" was always an expository song, not only introducing Corny Collins and all the Council kids but letting us know that they're not, actually, very nice. The movie's innovation (taking off from John Waters's own approach) is to cut back and forth between TV studio where the song is being performed, and the Turnblad living room, where Tracy and Penny are watching and dancing along to it on TV.

Velma's big number, "Miss Baltimore Crabs," demonstrates what can be done in a movie that can't happen on stage. "On stage, it's a confessional about her past and works brilliantly that way," says Zadan. "But Adam, working with Marc Shaiman and Scott Wittman, has made it a new number. It accomplishes the same thing lyrically—she's telling you about her past. But she's also teaching dance routines and auditioning the new kids. So Michelle Pfeiffer has the opportunity to give not only a tour de force of singing and dancing, but also an acting performance that fills in every blank about that character's

past, present and future." Film allows the scene to move back and forth in time easily, and into a fantasy dimension as well, the sets and costumes morphing with each stop along the way.

"Ladies Choice" is a new number that essentially replaces two songs from the show: "It Takes Two" (a mid-tempo song Link sings in the TV studio) and "The Madison," another favorite from the show. Neither fit the new script, for different reasons, so Shaiman and Wittman wrote a new up-tempo, high-energy rocker for Link to sing at the record hop. It advances the story, notes Zadan, "by showing the new steps Tracy's learned from Seaweed." And, Dixon adds, "it gives the kids a chance to really dance their asses off."

"New Girl in Town," written for the Broadway show, never made it to the stage but perfectly served the film's needs "to underscore a montage I did of Tracy's rise to stardom," says Dixon. It also serves another subplot, because Shankman shot it two ways: first as sung by Amber and her friends, then more dynamically by the Dynamites, a black girl group who wrote the song.

In the stage production, "Welcome to the Sixties" was a modest-sized number, but in the new film, says Zadan, "it is a complete renovation—an enormous song and dance number for Edna. Because we wanted to utilize John Travolta to the fullest." The song's impact is enhanced, Dixon thinks, because of how Edna is portrayed in this interpretation. "I wanted to take Edna from a quivering, beaten-down, overweight housewife to somebody who could embrace feminism and get involved in Tracy's cause. She's a laundress, and our concept was that she hasn't been out of the house in 10 years. Now when she comes out for 'Welcome to the Sixties,' it's a bigger deal."

"Run and Tell That" takes us on another journey through town. "We travel with Seaweed and the other kids from the school, onto the bus, to Maybelle's place," says Zadan. "And through that journey, we learn about who they are and what their lives are like and what their goals are. It just transports you. It's constantly moving."

"Big, Blonde and Beautiful" went through a complete makeover thanks to a new plotline—and Michelle Pfeiffer. Originally sung by Maybelle, it's now reprised twice with very different meanings: first by Velma, then by Edna a little later. This came about because Pfeiffer, reading the new seduction scene, wondered "Why isn't it musicalized?" As Zadan recalls, "By the end of that day, Adam had the answer. We'll make it a number that Velma sings while getting

ready to seduce Wilbur. And Edna sings the counterpoint while she's getting ready to seduce her husband. We cut back and forth between both women focusing on this guy, who doesn't have a clue what's going on."

With "Timeless to Me," "we went way beyond what happened on stage, which was beautiful and touching," says Zadan. "We had Travolta and Chris Walken, two song-and-dance men, and Adam choreographed a great dance number for them." Again, the scene morphs into fantasy as Edna and Wilbur dance in their backyard, first in their own clothes, then in a steamy tango, then in full Fred-and-Ginger ballroom regalia. This song suggested to Leslie Dixon that Wilbur should be "more woven into the plot. So I made him the target of an evil seduction attempt by Velma, which wreaks havoc in the Turnblad household. In a stage musical, characters can be happy all the time, and it's fine. In a movie, everything has to go wrong until it goes right in the very last frame. I wanted there to be some problems in the marriage so that lovely song could be their reconciliation."

"I Know Where I've Been" is another song that goes on a journey. In the musical, Motormouth Maybelle sings this deeply emotional, dramatic song from one spot on the stage, and it's a showstopper. But on film, it doesn't work for the performer to plant her feet and sing for five minutes. So in the movie her song became the rallying cry for a civil rights march that starts at a church and moves on to the TV station, transporting viewers through streets and alleys and buildings. "That can only happen in a movie musical," says Zadan.

"Without Love" is a storytelling song that brings us through many plot elements, says Zadan. "It's built into little blocks that progress the story. Rather than through dialogue, it's told through these components of the musical number." In the show, Dixon explains, Links helps Tracy break out of jail, they kiss, and the romantic climax occurs too soon. "I wanted to keep them physically apart until the very last. Now they're singing that they love each other, but in different locations; they can't be together because she's a fugitive. But this is the lovely thing about a movie: you can have him sing a line in one location, and cut to her singing a line in another. They're thinking about each other, still doing the duet, and nothing is lost."

Songwriters Shaiman and Wittman had in mind the great mid-sixties duets by Marvin Gaye and Tammy Tyrrel in writing "Without Love." Notes Shaiman, "Tracy and Penny and Seaweed are forward thinkers. When they do this song,

they feel what's coming in the future, and you can hear it."

The last song cut from the film was "Big Doll House," which takes place in the jail after Tracy and friends are arrested. In the film, Tracy escapes instead. "When you're dealing with movie reality, breaking someone out of jail is an elaborate process," says Dixon. "I didn't want to turn this into an intricate heist to spring Tracy; I wanted to spend time on other things."

"Finding the most cinematic way to tell the story is what these musical numbers have accomplished," says Zadan.

Next morning, Tracy's parents find her bed empty. She's left to join the crowd gathered outside a church to march on TV station WYZT. Though Maybelle warns her that she'll pay a price for what she's doing, Tracy doesn't care. As the marchers sweep through Baltimore's streets, Maybelle sings "*I Know Where I've Been.*" Tracy and others add their voices as more and more people join the procession ... including, finally, Edna, who shows up to take Tracy home but gets caught up in the moment. Velma, alerted to what's going on, plots with the police chief to make the protesters unwelcome. When they reach the station, a sergeant rudely rebuffs Maybelle ... and when Tracy intervenes, he tries to arrest her. Tracy escapes along with some of the marchers, but many are carted off to jail. Among them is Edna, who objects to being treated better than the black people around her. "You apologize to these people," she demands in her Mom voice, "and let them go home to their families this minute!" Eventually they do get to go home ... but only because Wilbur bails everyone out.

"'I Know Where I've Been' harks back to a moment in the John Waters movie where the kids go and dance on black side. At the record shop there's a soul singer doing a kind of Sam Cooke/'Change Is Gonna Come' number. John was great at finding the perfect songs for his score. Both that song and our song for Maybelle, which was born of the same style, point up this longing for change. It's the only serious ballad in the score, with real heart and soul to it."
— Composer Marc Shaiman

"I Know Where I've Been"

There's a dream in the future
there's a struggle we have yet to win
And I know where I've been...

There's a road we must travel
There's a promise we must make
But the riches will be plenty worth the risk
and the chances that we take

Hairspray Gets Serious

The story of *Hairspray*, in essence, is the John Waters version of reality. It's what should have happened. There was a real TV dance show in his youth, and there was pressure to integrate it—beyond the one day a month when black kids could come and dance by themselves. But it didn't happen the way he eventually wrote it. As Waters tells it:

"It went something like this: Buddy Deane was an exclusively white show. Once a month the show was all black … so the NAACP targeted the show for protests. Ironically, the show introduced black music and artists into the lives of white Baltimore teenagers, many of whom learned to dance from black friends and listened to black radio. Buddy offered to have three or even four days a week all black, but that wasn't it. The protesters wanted the races to mix.

"At frantic meetings of the Committee [the show's regular dancers], many said, 'My parents simply won't let me come if it's integrated,' and WJZ realized it just couldn't be done. 'It was the times,' most remember. 'This town just wasn't ready for that.' There were threats and bomb scares; integrationists smuggled whites into the all-black shows to dance cheek to cheek on camera with blacks, and that was it. *The Buddy Deane Show* was over."

The *Hairspray* 2007 filmmakers, while never losing their comedic focus, made sure that Waters's message lost none of its impact. Screenwriter Leslie Dixon says, "Even in the original film and the stage production there is a more serious story about integration, and what blacks were going through in 1962. Without sacrificing any of the fun of the piece, I think we've pushed that story forward a bit. As in Tracy's mother and father becoming more involved in that story, and getting invested in it."

Similarly, the hateful behavior of Velma was emphasized. "She says truly horrible things to Maybelle; things that would make her a pariah these days. But in 1962, you can tell a woman that her demographic is cleaning ladies and lawn jockeys, and get away with it. I wanted the audience to despise her."

Adam Shankman is grateful for the chance "to make a really arch comedy about something serious. "Racism simply hasn't gone away, or a lot of the ways people judge others for all the wrong reasons. And people having dreams of equality and acceptance hasn't gone away either.

He describes his approach to the material as a hybrid. "As a director I make sunny, sweet fare—usually I'm not dealing with something as thematically important as this. I always want to feel how much both worlds have in

common—about dancing and hanging out and music. The kids mostly are colorblind and nonjudgmental, except Amber, who's a victim of the times.

"So in one way, my approach is just to heighten the celebration. But at the same time, this movie pushes the racism card harder. It's one thing to say some of the things in the Broadway show on a stage, when people are far away. To watch people say those things in closeup can be rough. It's daring to take a comedic approach to something so incredibly unfunny.

"There is nothing funny about prejudice," he elaborates, "but there is something really funny and ridiculous about people who are prejudiced. And anytime I can put a mirror up to those people and say: Look at who you are, look at what you do, look at how you hurt people—and boy, do you look foolish doing it— I'm a happy guy."

Shankman especially cherished the role Queen Latifah played. "She is, like Motormouth Maybelle, a one-woman NAACP. She stands for everything that's right and nonjudgmental and optimistic about being ethnic. Understanding that people are afraid of change, and are ridiculous, and you really can't worry about them."

Says Queen Latifah, "But I love what's going on in the film, what we're dealing with. Finding the energy of change and how change will only happen if you push it along. It's not going to happen by just sitting around talking about it. You have to do something."

1962 Timeline
Martin Luther King, Jr.

*T*he background: King recognized that organized, nonviolent protest against segregation and Jim Crow laws would produce extensive media coverage of the struggle for black equality and voting rights. Journalistic accounts and televised footage of the indignities suffered by Southern blacks, and of violence and harassment of civil rights workers and marchers, produced a wave of sympathetic public opinion that made the Civil Rights Movement the most important issue in American politics in the early 1960s. King organized and led marches for blacks' right to vote, desegregation, labor rights and other basic civil rights. Most of these rights were successfully enacted into law with the passage of the Civil Rights Act of 1964 and the Voting Rights Act of 1965. (source: Wikipedia)

February 27
Dr. King is tried and convicted for leading the December march in Albany, Georgia.

May 2
Dr. King is invited to join protests in Birmingham, Alabama.

July 27
Dr. King is arrested at an Albany, Georgia, city hall prayer vigil and jailed on charges of failure to obey a police officer, obstructing the sidewalk, and disorderly conduct.

September 20
James Meredith makes his first attempt to enroll at the University of Mississippi. He is enrolled by Supreme Court order and escorted onto the Oxford, Mississippi, campus by U.S. Marshals on October 1, 1962.

October 16
Dr. King meets with President John F. Kennedy at the White House for a one-hour conference.

"There is nothing funny about prejudice, but there is something really funny and ridiculous about people who are prejudiced. And anytime I can put a mirror up to those people and say: Look at who you are, look at what you do, look at how you hurt people—and boy, do you look foolish doing it— I'm a happy guy."
— Adam Shankman

*T*racy's on the lam, and Edna is frantic. That night Penny watches the evening news and sees her friend fleeing the police ... and just then, Tracy's face appears at her window. Penny hides her in the Pingletons' air-raid shelter, but Prudy discovers them. She calls the cops on Tracy and locks Penny in her room. But the police are busy tracking down false leads called in by Tracy's parents and others to throw them off her trail. ... Link, realizing how much he cares, shows up at the Turnblads' full of regrets. Although parted, with Tracy in the basement and Link in her bedroom, they both sing "*Without Love.*" Meanwhile, Seaweed comes to Penny's rescue. These lovebirds join in the duet, and then spring Tracy from her prison in the nick of time. Seaweed's friends are waiting outside, and Prudy watches in horror as her daughter drives off "in a car full of Negroes!" And no seatbelts, either!

Prudy
That Tracy Turnblad always was
a bad influence! You will never
see that beehived
harlot again!

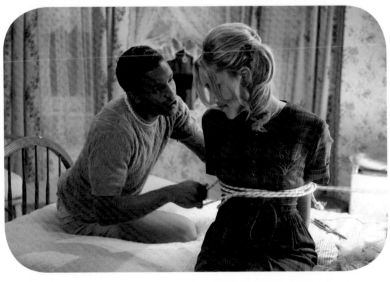

Do You Remember....?
Elvis in 1962

March/April
Elvis records and films in Hollywood, and does location filming in Hawaii for his eleventh movie, *Girls! Girls! Girls!*

May/June
Follow That Dream opens nationally to warm reviews, and reaches number five in box office.

July
Priscilla Beaulieu, age 17, flies from Germany to Los Angeles to see Elvis, their first reunion since his Army discharge in 1960.

August/September
Elvis records and films for his twelfth movie, *It Happened at the World's Fair*, shooting in Hollywood and on location at the Seattle World's Fair. *Kid Galahad* opens nationally and does relatively well, with a brief stay in the box office top ten.

October
In Mexico, riots in a theater showing *GI Blues* prompts the Mexican government to ban Elvis movies.

November
Girls! Girls! Girls! opens nationally and rivals *Blue Hawaii* in box office success. The soundtrack album goes top five and yields the hit single "Return to Sender."

December
Priscilla spends the Christmas holidays with Elvis at Graceland, moving there in early 1963 and completing her senior year of high school in Memphis.

Tracy
I think I've kind of been in a bubble … thinking that fairness was gonna just happen. It's not. People like me are gonna have to get up … and go out and fight for it.

"Without Love"

Without love
Life is like the seasons with no summer
Without love
life is rock 'n' roll without a drummer.

Without love
life is like a beat that you can't follow
Without love
life is Doris Day at the Apollo

Maybelle

Well, love is a gift. But not everyone remembers that. So you two better brace yourselves for a whole lot of ugly comin' at you from a never-ending parade of stupid.

Do You Remember....?
James Brown at the Apollo

One of the legendary performances in pop went down on a cold October night in 1962, when James Brown played a headline date at Harlem's Apollo Theater—his seventh at the famed venue. Built in 1913, the Apollo since 1934 had hosted a weekly amateur night that introduced the young Ella Fitzgerald, among others including Lena Horne, Sam Cooke, and Marvin Gaye. It was also a popular site for live recordings, seasoned with the spicy audience-performer dialogue that was a feature of the place.

Over the objections of his label, Brown insisted on taping the show, paying for the recording himself. It went on to become known as one of the greatest and best-selling live albums ever recorded, with Brown and his band ripping through 30 minutes' worth of the star's popular cuts in a tightly controlled frenzy. A spectacular stage performer, Brown also knew how to put together a set to maximum effect. Songs on the album, reissued on CD in 2004, include "Are You Ready for Star Time?", the 1958 hit "Try Me," and "Lost Someone." Brown went on to even wider recognition during his funk period in the later sixties, but to some aficionados, this was his peak.

Roadblocks have been set up around Baltimore to catch Tracy, and Seaweed's car is stopped. The cops peer inside, but no Tracy. She's hidden in the trunk ... and still singing. Finally the escapees reach Maybelle's place, where the song reaches its frenetic climax. Once Maybelle figures out what's going on, she gives her blessing to Seaweed and Penny but warns them they're in for a rough time. And she gladly takes in the fugitive. Tracy calls home to tell Edna and Wilbur she's okay. She's going to need their help for the contest tomorrow.

It's the big day at last! An all-white crowd pours into the WYZT studio for the Miss Teenage Hairspray finals, a TV crew filming the action. Corny Collins warms the crowd up with the "Hairspray" theme song as the votes are tallied. Amber now leads Tracy by a few points ... but only because Velma is collecting the tally cards and stealthily switching them with fake ones. Outside, swarms of police and reporters are on the lookout for Tracy. Everyone figures she'll have to show up to stop Amber from winning. The dance-off begins, with Amber giving her all, and still no sign of Tracy ... until the cops spot a familiar figure from behind and swoop down to grab the culprit. But it's Wilbur, disguised as Tracy to create a diversion while her friends infiltrate the studio. Once the cops haul Wilbur back outside, they find themselves locked out ... Tracy's gang has barricaded the doors from inside!

Corny

And now, broadcast in front of a live studio audience... it's the event of a lifetime... the crescendo of a young girl's dream... it's the Corny Collins Miss Teenage Hairspray pageant!

Local Anchorman
And this is live at WYZT, where the Miss Teenage Hairspray pageant has just been interrupted by the surprise illegal entry of fugitive Tracy Turnblad, whose imminent arrest we should be seeing in just a few moments... or maybe a few more bars...

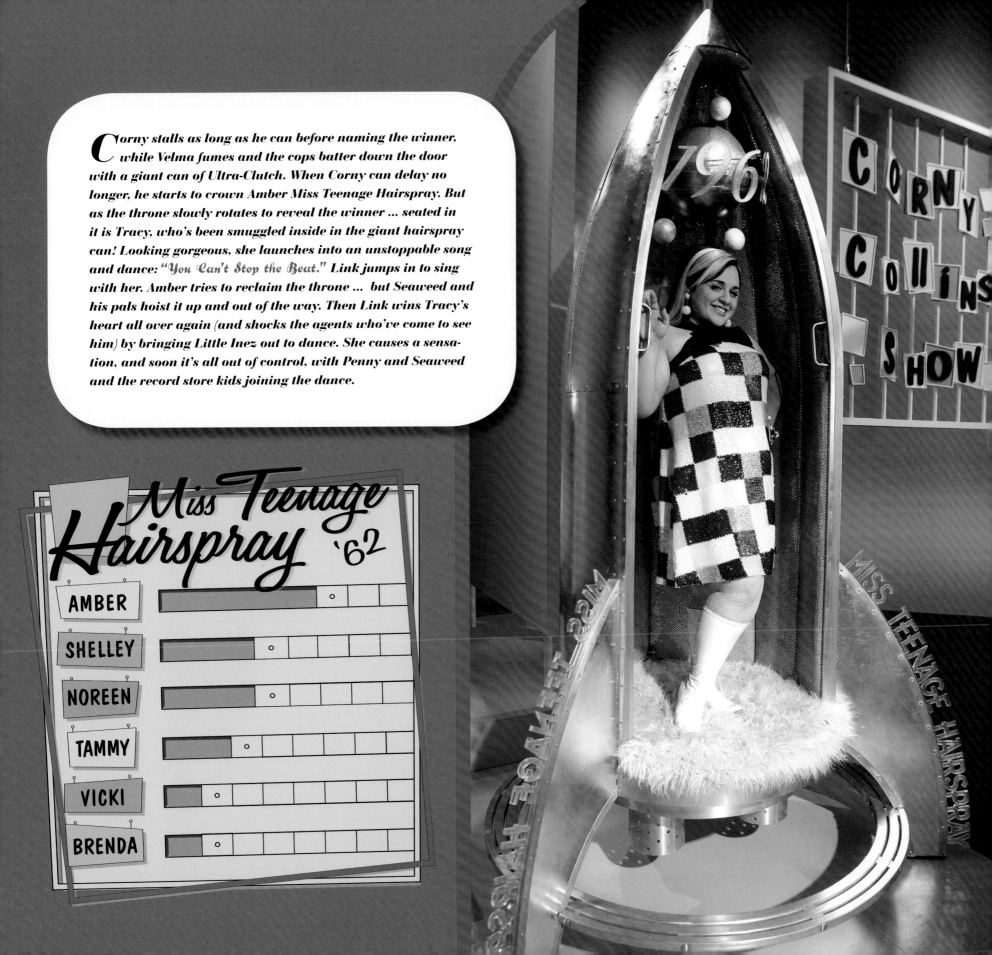

Corny stalls as long as he can before naming the winner, while Velma fumes and the cops batter down the door with a giant can of Ultra-Clutch. When Corny can delay no longer, he starts to crown Amber Miss Teenage Hairspray. But as the throne slowly rotates to reveal the winner ... seated in it is Tracy, who's been smuggled inside in the giant hairspray can! Looking gorgeous, she launches into an unstoppable song and dance: "You Can't Stop the Beat." Link jumps in to sing with her. Amber tries to reclaim the throne ... but Seaweed and his pals hoist it up and out of the way. Then Link wins Tracy's heart all over again (and shocks the agents who've come to see him) by bringing Little Inez out to dance. She causes a sensation, and soon it's all out of control, with Penny and Seaweed and the record store kids joining the dance.

Miss Teenage Hairspray '62

- AMBER
- SHELLEY
- NOREEN
- TAMMY
- VICKI
- BRENDA

"You Can't Stop the Beat"

You can't stop an avalanche
as it races down the hill
You can try to stop the seasons, girl,
but you know you never will
And you can try to stop my dancing feet
But I just cannot stand still

Hairspray Part Two

*N*ow comes the real surprise: Corny announces that a surge of late voting has chosen a new contest winner – Little Inez Stubbs! Which also makes her the new lead dancer on his show, integrating it officially and forever. Velma goes ballistic, screaming that Amber can't have lost because "I switched the damn tally!!" Oops ... the TV camera is recording Velma's tirade, and Mr. Spritzer promptly fires her. The singing and dancing build to a crescendo, with Edna and Maybelle taking their turns in the spotlight. Finally the Police Chief gives in, rips up his warrant for Tracy, and arrests Velma instead. It's obvious to him and to everyone that *"You can't stop the beat!"*

You can't stop the motion of the ocean
or the rain from above
You can try to stop the paradise
we're dreamin' of
But you cannot stop the rhythm
of two hearts in love to stay
'Cause you can't stop the beat!

Corny

Baltimore, you have picked a winner... Inez Stubbs, congratulations!... This also makes you the lead dancer on the Corny Collins Show. The Corny Collins Show is now and forever officially integrated!

Thirteen-year-old Taylor Parks has a role that starts out small but ends up big, as Little Inez Stubbs—Seaweed's baby sister—who wins the Miss Hairspray pageant, in a surprise twist. Parks diligently did her homework for the film, studying up on the civil rights era as well as attending to her dance studies with extra effort. She has performed at the Kennedy Center in an original dance musical written and directed by Debbie Allen, with whom she studies. And she has several TV and film roles to her credit.

But *Hairspray* was definitely her most challenging role to date. In the finale, she has to do some of the most strenuous dancing of any cast member in the show. "Doing the flip over Zac's back took a lot of work," she laughs. "The choreographers trained me, and then stood behind me when I practiced so I didn't fall on my face. It was pretty scary at first, with my dress flying everywhere. But I got used to it."

Just as star-struck as anyone on the cast or crew, she says that her famous colleagues treated her like one of them. With Elijah Kelley, who plays Seaweed, she developed close ties. "He brightens up the set—even when it's 12 at night, here Elijah comes, and it's 'Let's go, everybody let's go!'" Seaweed and Inez have a pretty good relationship, she says "but sometimes Inez will tease him about having a girlfriend, like a normal little sister."

Queen Latifah was the performer she most looked up to, no surprise. "She's playful, and she'll talk to everybody," says Parks. "And she will make you drop to your knees laughing. So if I could make her laugh, I feel like I'm hilarious. Like, wow, I just made Queen Latifah laugh."

Parks, who celebrated her 13th birthday on the set, says, "Being cast in this part—this is my birthday present right here."

*Ever since this old world began
A woman found out if she shook it
she could shake up a man
And so I'm gonna shake and shimmy it
the best I can today
'cause you can't stop the motion of the ocean
or the sun in the sky
You can wonder if you wanna
but I never ask why
And if you try to hold me down
I'm gonna spit in your eye and say
you can't stop the beat!*

It's All About the Dancing

Words, spoken or sung, tell part of the *Hairspray* story, but much of its action and character development unfold through dancing. Adam Shankman made careful choices about what the choreography needed to convey—in particular, to distinguish between the dance styles of the white kids versus "specifically authentic black sixties dancing," says Craig Zadan.

"The music made me do it," says Adam Shankman about his choreography. "The music and lyrics are so powerful, filled with joy and emotion and all the stuff that we should be thinking about." Shankman started out as a dancer and had worked as a choreographer on many films, but since graduating to the director's chair he hadn't had the chance to work on a movie musical. The time was ripe and the material perfectly suited to his dance sensibilities. "Maybe because of the nature of the story, maybe because I hadn't choreographed much for six or seven years, the steps just kind of poured out of me," he says. "I made way more dancing than there is even in the Broadway show."

Shankman's dance background guided all his important choices on the film, he says. "I always knew that in the brain of this movie, music and dancing should be going on constantly—because that's what Tracy has going on in her head constantly."

As the film's choreographer, Shankman also had the task of hiring a crack corps of dancers to portray the Council Kids, the Detention Kids, and assorted other participants in the big numbers. "It was a little daunting because I had requested a lot of dancers: 135 in total. And I added ten council members to the original group, so twenty of those. Plus about ten or twelve Detention kids and all the Maybelle dancers. I wanted them all to have different movement vocabularies, so the audition process was a little crazy."

Shankman saw about 2,200 dancers in New York, L.A. and Toronto to identify those 135. "The auditions were like parties; everybody was so into it, cheering each other on. The kids I ended up casting might not in every case be the very best dancers I saw, but all of them are the right dancers for the movie."

Plotting out the numbers, getting the steps onto the actors' and dancers' bodies, and polishing it all in rehearsal before the shoot was a huge undertaking—especially since Shankman had to wear his director's hat as well. He was well supported by associate choreographers Anne Fletcher, Joey Pizzi, Zach Woodlee, and Jamal Simms.

Shankman had known Fletcher since they met while both were dancing on the Oscars telecast in 1990. She later became his assistant, then went on to choreograph and direct on her own. "Anne—we call her Mama—had just come off directing *Step Up*, which I produced, so I got to watch her graduate to that next thing. I think she's going to go off and be a big director. We'll always be best friends, though." Pizzi had worked with producers Zadan and Meron on *Chicago* and later was an associate choreographer on *Dreamgirls*; Woodlee's extensive dance credits include *Step Up*, on which he was also assistant choreographer.

Shankman and Fletcher started their work in a Los Angeles studio. "Then we had Joey and Zac come, started teaching them the steps," says Shankman. "Jamal joined us a little later. I would choreograph things and explain how I wanted it to be different for the Detention kids and the Maybelle kids. Jamal has choreographed for Usher and he's done a lot of urban material, so he would show me how something would look done in a more urban way."

Elijah Kelley describes how this was expressed in the Detention kids' dancing. "We're a little bit looser, just more hip and cool. The white kids are supposed to look more stiff, right on the count, kind of prissy. In "Ladies' Choice," we're actually doing the same dance but it looks like two totally different dances."

Of that number Zadan says, "The choreography's amazing. And it's also very disturbing because there's a rope down the center of the gym. The black kids have to dance on one side and the white kids on the other side. So although you're watching a fun, jubilant musical number, you're always reminded of the divide, of what's forbidden. It's pointing out something without preaching."

The choreography team brought in a skeleton crew of dancers while still on the West Coast, and also worked with some of the young actors who had lots of steps to learn. Then the whole show moved to Toronto for the main rehearsal period. The featured actors were endlessly grateful for the choreographers' care and feeding of them. John Travolta notes: "Adam's guys were brilliant about duplicating exactly what he wanted, so he never worried too much when we were off working on a number. And he would allow us freedom to tweak it, so I could add my interpretation. Basically, his whole movie was choreographed before any of us got there. It was a matter of his team teaching the cast, and then Adam quality-checking it at the end of the day, to see how we were progressing."

Says Brittany Snow, "Because it is a dance movie, the choreographers have a lot of input on our characters. We got really close with them because they

"To do a comedy with a message like this, to stage and interpret these wonderful songs … this movie's just a revelation for me personally. The choreography just kind of poured out of me."
— Adam Shankman

were with us from the beginning, and they help us so much. Most of us in the cast—we dance, but we're not professional dancers. We look to them to make sure we're getting it across exactly right."

One number that wasn't all worked out in advance was the big finale, "You Can't Stop the Beat." Recalls Shankman, "It was just such a puzzle—figuring out who's dancing when and what is Edna's dance versus Maybelle's dance; and let's lock up the von Tussles' part, and on and on. There's so much song, and it just grew and grew."

A high point of that number, and one of Shankman's favorite moments in

the movie, is the dance break he created for Travolta. "John had this idea that he wanted Edna to be sort of like Tina Turner there … maybe because I said that I wanted him in a minidress," says the director. "So we came up with a movement vocabulary for that dance break, which I think the audience is really going to love. He's in a minidress with those big old legs, shaking it all over the place … out there dancing with forty-five kids like he's one of them." Observes Craig Zadan, "It's where Edna crosses over to the other side."

"The first time we see John in the dress, it's long. He looks like an opera diva. And then he rips away the skirt and suddenly he's in a mini-dress. So that's showing Edna's liberation."
— Costume designer Rita Ryack

"You Can't Stop the Beat"

You can't stop today
as it comes speeding down the track
Child, yesterday is history
and it's never coming back
'Cause tomorrow is a brand new day
and it don't know white from black
'Cause the world keeps spinning
round and round
and my heart's keeping time
to the speed of sound
I was lost till I heard the drums,
then I found my way
'Cause you can't stop the beat!

NEW LINE CINEMA
A Time Warner Company

presents

in association with Ingenious Film Partners

a Zadan/Meron production

an Adam Shankman film

John Travolta *as* Edna Turnblad
Michelle Pfeiffer *as* Velma Von Tussle
Christopher Walken *as* Wilbur Turnblad
Amanda Bynes *as* Penny Pingleton
James Marsden *as* Corny Collins
and Queen Latifah *as* Motormouth Maybelle

HAIRSPRAY

Brittany Snow *as* Amber Von Tussle
Zac Efron *as* Link Larson
Allison Janney *as* Prudy Pingleton
Elijah Kelley *as* Seaweed J. Stubbs
and introducing
Nikki Blonsky *as* Tracy Turnblad

Casting by David Rubin, C.S.A.
and Richard Hicks, C.S.A.

Based on the 1988 Screenplay "Hairspray" written
by John Waters and 2002 Musical stage play "Hairspray"

Book by Mark O'Donnell Thomas Meehan
Music by Marc Shaiman
Lyrics by Scott Wittman Marc Shaiman
Music Score by Marc Shaiman
Songs: Music by Marc Shaiman
Lyrics by Scott Wittman and Marc Shaiman
Costume Designer Rita Ryack
Edited by Michael Tronick, A.C.E.
Production Designer David Gropman
Director of Photography Bojan Bazelli

Executive Producers
Adam Shankman Jennifer Gibgot Garrett Grant
Executive Producers
Toby Emmerich Mark Kaufman Marc Shaiman
Scott Wittman
Executive Producers
Bob Shaye Michael Lynne
Produced by Craig Zadan Neil Meron
Screenplay by Leslie Dixon
Choreographed and Directed by Adam Shankman

www.hairspraymovie.com

About the Filmmakers

ADAM SHANKMAN (Director, Choreographer, Executive Producer) made his directorial debut in 2001 with the hit feature *The Wedding Planner*. His subsequent string of successes includes *A Walk to Remember, Bringing Down the House, The Pacifier,* and *Cheaper by the Dozen 2*. He most recently executive produced 2006's sleeper hit, *Step Up*, and has also directed for the hit television series *Monk*.

Shankman and his sister, producer Jennifer Gibgot, formed Offspring Entertainment in 2003, with an overall deal that they recently renewed at Disney. They have several high-profile comedies in development including a retelling of *Topper*, starring Steve Martin with Mandeville Films with Shankman attached to direct.

Prior to directing, Shankman was one of the entertainment world's premiere dance and physical comedy choreographers, putting his creative stamp on many well-known comedies, dramas, thrillers, and animated films including *The Addams Family, Casper, Inspector Gadget, Anastasia, George of the Jungle, Boogie Nights, Miami Rhapsody* and *The Flintstones*, for which he was nominated for a Bob Fosse Award. Shankman won the Bob Fosse award for his work with Simon West. At age 24, Shankman teamed up with influential video director Julian Temple as a music video choreographer; for example, on Whitney Houston's *I'm Your Baby Tonight*. He has also choreographed videos for the B-52's, Barry White, Aaron Neville, Chic and Stevie Wonder.

A native of Los Angeles, where he currently resides, Shankman moved to New York after high school and attended Juilliard in the dance program for two years. After five years of work as an actor and dancer in New York and regional theater, he moved back to Los Angeles and began dancing in music videos, including videos for Paula Abdul and Janet Jackson. He also performed at the 1989 Academy Awards.

CRAIG ZADAN and **NEIL MERON** (Producers), under their Storyline Entertainment banner, are the producers of critically acclaimed and award-winning feature films, television movies and series. Their films and television movies have garnered a total of six Academy Awards, five Golden Globes, eleven Emmy Awards, and two Peabodys, among other recognition. Their movies for television have amassed sixty-six Emmy nominations.

Their feature film *Chicago*, which they executive produced for Miramax, was nominated for thirteen Academy Awards, winning six including Best Picture of the Year. Nominated for seven Golden Globes, the film won three, including Best Motion Picture - Musical or Comedy. *Chicago* received many other nominations and awards, including a Grammy for Best Motion Picture Soundtrack of the Year and went on to become Miramax's highest-grossing movie in the studio's history and the first movie musical in 34 years to win the best picture Oscar.

Zadan and Meron have produced several landmark musical films for television: *Gypsy*, starring Better Midler, which was nominated for twelve Emmys and won a Golden Globe for Bette Midler; *Rodgers & Hammerstein's Cinderella*, starring Whitney Houston, Brandy and Whoopi Goldberg, which was the highest-rated television

film in fourteen years and garnered seven Emmy nominations; *Annie*, starring Kathy Bates, which won two Emmys; and *Meredith Willson's The Music Man* starring Matthew Broderick and Kristin Chenoweth, which received five Emmy nominations.

Their television credits also include comedies and dramatic films: *The Reagans*, starring James Brolin and Judy Davis, which received seven Emmy nominations; *Martin and Lewis*, starring Sean Hayes and Jeremy Northam; *What Makes A Family*, starring Brooke Shields, Cherry Jones, and Whoopi Goldberg; *Serving in Silence: The Margarethe Cammermeyer Story*, starring Glenn Close and Judy Davis, which won three Emmys; *Life With Judy Garland: Me and My Shadows*, starring Judy Davis, which won five Emmys and a Golden Globe for Judy Davis; *The Beach Boys: An American Family*, nominated for three Emmys; and a new version of the classic *Brian's Song* for The Wonderful World of Disney.

They recently executive produced Lorraine Hansberry's *A Raisin in the Sun* for ABC, starring Sean Combs, Phylicia Rashad, Audra MacDonald, and Sanaa Lathan. This three-hour television event will air in 2008. Their next movie musical for television is going to be the first film version of the classic musical *Peter Pan* for ABC.

Their next feature film release will be *The Bucket List* for Warner Bros. starring Jack Nicholson and Morgan Freeman, directed by Rob Reiner. Upcoming for the pair will be *The Mayor of Castro Street* for Warner Bros., to be directed by Bryan Singer. Previously for Warner Bros. they executive produced the feature comedy *My Fellow Americans* starring Jack Lemmon and James Garner.

Zadan's first feature film production was Paramount Picture's *Footloose*, starring Kevin Bacon and John Lithgow, nominated for two Academy Awards.

MARC SHAIMAN (Composer, Executive Producer) is a composer, lyricist, arranger and performer for films, television and theater. His film credits include *Broadcast News, Beaches, When Harry Met Sally..., City Slickers, The Addams Family, Sister Act, Sleepless in Seattle, A Few Good Men, The American President, The First Wives Club, George of the Jungle, In & Out, Patch Adams, South Park: Bigger Longer & Uncut* and HBO's *From The Earth To The Moon* and *61**. He has also appeared in many of these films.

Shaiman has earned five Academy Award nominations, a Tony Award and a Grammy Award for his work on the stage musical *Hairspray*, and an Emmy Award for co-writing Billy Crystal's Academy Award performances. He has also been Grammy nominated twice for his arrangements for Harry Connick, Jr.'s recordings *When Harry Met Sally* and *We Are In Love* and Emmy nominated for his work on *Saturday Night Live*. In 2002, he was honored with the Outstanding Achievement in Music-In-Film Award at the Hollywood Film Festival and in 2007 was given ASCAP's Henry Mancini Career Achievement Award.

Fans of *Saturday Night Live* may recognize him as Skip St. Thomas, the accompanying pianist for the Sweeney Sisters.

Shaiman started his career as a theater/cabaret musical director. He then became vocal arranger for Bette Midler, eventually becoming her musical director and co-producer of many of her recordings, including *The Wind Beneath My Wings* and *From A Distance*. He helped create the material for her Emmy Award-winning performance on the penultimate *Tonight Show with Johnny Carson*.

Shaiman recently co-wrote and appeared on Broadway in *Martin Short: Fame Becomes Me*. He lives in both New York City and Los Angeles.

SCOTT WITTMAN (Lyricist, Executive Producer) received the Tony and Grammy Award for his work on the stage musical *Hairspray*. On Broadway, in concert, for film and television and in many a *boite*, Wittman has conceived, written and/or directed and collaborated with such talents as Kristin Chenoweth, Jayne County, Sandy Duncan, Christine Ebersole, Dame Edna, Annie Golden, Debbie Gravitte, the High-Heeled Women, Allison Janney, Madeline Kahn, Lainie Kazan, Laura Kenyon (as Lainie Kazan), Nathan Lane, Ute Lemper, Darlene Love, Patti LuPone, Lypsinka, Ann Magnuson, Andrea Martin, Lonette McKee, Mike Myers, Bette Midler, Sarah Jessica Parker, John Sex, Elaine Stritch, Bruce Vilanch, Rufus Wainwright, Raquel Welch and Holly Woodlawn.

Wittman is currently co-writing a Broadway musicalization of Steven Spielberg's film *Catch Me If You Can* with Terrence McNally and Marc Shaiman, and just co-wrote and directed *Martin Short: Fame Becomes Me* on Broadway.

Wittman saw John Waters's *Pink Flamingos* at the Elgin Theatre in 1973, and he has never been the same since.

GARRETT GRANT's (Executive Producer) film credits include two previous collaborations with director Adam Shankman – *The Pacifier* and *Cheaper by the Dozen 2* – as well as nine films with longtime collaborators Bobby and Peter Farrelly: *The Ringer, Stuck On You, Shallow Hal, Osmosis Jones, Say It Isn't So, Me, Myself & Irene, There's Something About Mary, Kingpin* and *Dumb and Dumber*. He also served as co-producer on *Like Mike* and as line producer for *The Locusts*. He was the unit production manager on *Freddy Got Fingered* and *Gun Shy* and served as production supervisor for *Beverly Hills Ninja*.

Grant began his film career as a location manager for such films as *Killing Zoe* and *Albino Alligator*, among others.

JENNIFER GIBGOT (Executive Producer) most recently produced this summer's sleeper hit, *Step Up*, as well as the upcoming *Premonition*. Her other recent credits as executive producer include *Cheaper by the Dozen 2* and *The Pacifier*.

Gibgot began her career as a producer running Tapestry Films in 1995. Over the course of her eight years at Tapestry, she set up numerous projects and produced

successful films such as *She's All That* and *The Wedding Planner*. Gibgot hired her brother Adam Shankman, already an established choreographer, to helm *The Wedding Planner* which ultimately launched his directing career.

In 2003, Shankman and Gibgot formed Offspring Entertainment and signed a first look deal at Disney, where they have set up and are developing several projects such as *Topper, The Other Guy, Overparenting, Jack of All Trades* and *Flight Risk*.

DAVID JAMES (Photographer) was born in England and started his career in the photo lab at MGM Studios. By the age of 20, he was shooting stills on movies, and he is recognized today as one of the film industry's most accomplished and respected photographers. James has worked with some of the leading directors in film, and his work on musicals includes *Fiddler on the Roof, Jesus Christ Superstar, Yentl, Chicago* and *Dreamgirls*. His photographs also have appeared on film posters and in magazines, newspapers, and eight books. He has been honored with several awards, including in 2006 the Film Publicist Award for Excellence in Still Photography. He now lives in California and travels the world in his work.

Colophon / Acknowledgments

Publisher & Creative Director: Raoul Goff
Executive Directors: Peter Beren and Michael Madden
Art Director: Iain R. Morris
Designer: Usana Shadday
Writer: Diana Landau
Managing Editor: Jennifer Gennari
Editorial Assistant: Sonia Vallabh
Press Supervisor: Noah Potkin

Insight Editions would also like to give a very special thank you to Mikayla Butchart, Gabe Ely and Valerie Reckert.

The writer and Insight Editions wish to thank the following for invaluable support in the preparation of this book:

David James, whose brilliant photographs are the heart and soul of this volume.

John Waters, for graciously sharing his thoughts about this new *Hairspray* in his foreword.

At Storyline Entertainment: Producer Craig Zadan, whose careful guidance at every phrase was simply indispensable; producer Neil Meron, and Laine Bateman. And to Craig Zadan and Neil Meron for their insightful introduction.

At Offspring Entertainment: Director-choreographer Adam Shankman for contributing his introduction and key feedback on content.

At New Line Cinema: Russell Schwartz, Clare Ann Conlon, Mark Kaufman, Michael Mulvahill, Dave Imhoff, and especially Ed Bolkus for guiding the project from start to finish. Also to Katy Leigh at Automat Pictures for help with transcripts.

And to the creative folk who worked on *Hairspray* and contributed their stories to the book, in particular: songwriters Marc Shaiman and Scott Wittman, director of photography Bojan Bazelli, hair designer Judi Cooper-Sealy, special makeup designer Tony Gardner, production designer David Gropman, and costume designer Rita Ryack.

In addition to those mentioned in his introduction, Adam Shankman especially wishes to thank Jimmy Badstibner, associate choreographers Joey Pizzi, Jamal Sims and Zach Woodlee; director of photography Bojan Bazelli, production designer David Gropman, costume designer Rita Ryack, and film editor Michael Tronick.

Finally, our deepest thanks to all the filmmakers for their amazing creative achievement in bringing *Hairspray* back to the big screen.